DISGUSTING HISTORY

THE SMELLIEST, DIRTIEST ERAS OF THE PAST 10,000 YEARS

CAPSTONE PRESS

a capstone imprint

Fact Finder Books are published by Capstone Press,
1710 Roe Crest Drive, North Mankato, Minnesota 56003.
www.capstonepub.com

Library of Congress Cataloging-in-Publication Data
Allen, Kathy.
Disgusting history : the smelliest, dirtiest eras of the past 10,000
years / by Kathy Allen, James A. Corrick, Christopher Forest, Kay
Melchisedech Olson, Elizabeth Raum, Heather E. Schwartz.
pages cm
Summary: "Describes the disgusting details about daily life in several
historical eras, including housing, food, and sanitation"— Provided
by publisher.
Includes index.
ISBN 978-1-4765-7745-6 (pbk.)
1. Culture—History—Juvenile literature. 2. Manners and customs—
Juvenile literature. 3. Civilization--History—Juvenile literature.
I. Title.

CB151.A596 2014
909—dc23 2013028668

Editorial Credits
Marissa Bolte and Christine Peterson, editors; Gene Bentdahl, Ashlee
Suker, and Alison Thiele, designers; Wanda Winch and Svetlana
Zurkin, media researchers; Eric Manske, production specialist

Printed in the United States of America in Stevens Point, Wisconsin.
102013   007810R

TABLE OF CONTENTS

CHAPTER ONE

GRITTY, STINKY ANCIENT EGYPT

ANCIENT EGYPT
3100–30 BC

PAGE 11

3100–2700 BC

Narmer unites Upper and Lower Egypt. Memphis is the capital. Writing in the form of hieroglyphs appears.

2625 BC

The Old Kingdom begins.

THE GREAT PYRAMID BY THE NUMBERS

57,000,000 TONS (51,710,000 METRIC TONS)—total weight

23,000,000—approximate number of blocks

2.5 TONS (2.3 METRIC TONS)—average weight of one block

15 TONS (13.6 METRIC TONS)—weight of the largest block

756 FEET (230 METERS)—length of the pyramid's base on one side

13.1 ACRES (5.3 HECTARES)—total area of the pyramid's base

481.3 FEET (146.7 METERS)—the pyramid's original height

PAGE 9

2589–2566 BC

Pharaoh Khufu rules and builds the Great Pyramid at Giza.

2181 BC

The Old Kingdom ends.

MILLIONS OF MUMMIES

It has been estimated that more than 70 million mummies were made during the time of the pharaohs.

2055 BC

The Middle Kingdom begins. Its capital is Thebes.

1550 BC

The New Kingdom begins.

1650 BC

The Middle Kingdom comes to an end.

PAGE 30

1650–1550 BC

Hyksos invaders conquer and rule much of Egypt. They bring the chariot to Egypt.

1279–1213 BC

Pharaoh Ramses II rules Egypt.

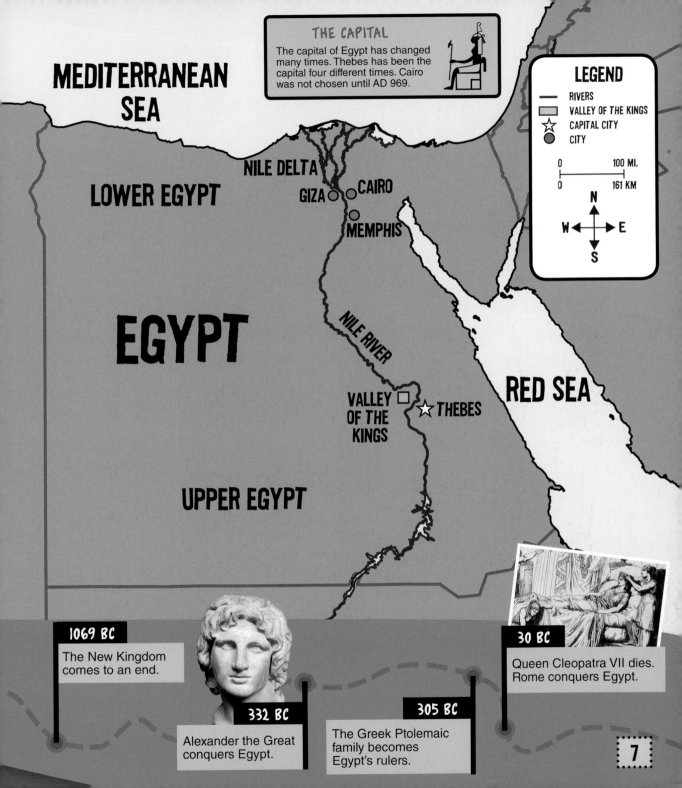

MEDITERRANEAN SEA

THE CAPITAL
The capital of Egypt has changed many times. Thebes has been the capital four different times. Cairo was not chosen until AD 969.

LEGEND

——	RIVERS
▢	VALLEY OF THE KINGS
☆	CAPITAL CITY
●	CITY

0   100 MI.
0   161 KM

N
W ✛ E
S

NILE DELTA

LOWER EGYPT

GIZA ○ CAIRO
○
● MEMPHIS

EGYPT

NILE RIVER

RED SEA

VALLEY OF THE KINGS ▢ ☆ THEBES

UPPER EGYPT

1069 BC
The New Kingdom comes to an end.

332 BC
Alexander the Great conquers Egypt.

305 BC
The Greek Ptolemaic family becomes Egypt's rulers.

30 BC
Queen Cleopatra VII dies. Rome conquers Egypt.

ANCIENT HISTORY

Ancient Egypt is known for its pyramids, pharaohs, and, of course, mummies! But it was also a place where backbreaking labor, deadly illnesses, and dirty rivers were common. For about 3,000 years, ancient Egyptians toiled under the hot sun. Pyramids had to be built. Mummies had to be made. And sand from the Sahara desert got in everything.

Ancient Egyptians lived along the banks of the Nile River. The river waters were polluted with human and animal waste.

Dangerous animals called the river home too. Hungry crocodiles lived along the river's banks, waiting for an unsuspecting person or animal to get too close.

During the flooding season, no farming could be done. Instead, the pharaoh required men to build the pyramids. They were not paid. Their work was seen as a service to the pharaoh and his family. Men worked for eight days and then rested for the next two days. Sometimes they were given free days for holidays. Other times they were given time off to work on their own tombs. Leaders liked to keep the peasants busy year-round. They thought that if their subjects were working, there would be less time for boredom and making trouble.

Nearly 70 pyramids were built around Cairo.

THE WORKING CLASSES

Who's the boss? In ancient Egypt, it was the pharaoh. Most pharaohs were men, but a few were women. The pharaoh was believed to be the earthly form of Horus, the Egyptian sky god.

After the pharaoh and his family, Egyptian society had three main classes. At the top were the rich nobles, who included governors and priests. They held most of the land and wealth. Below them were the artists and educated men. This class included doctors, lawyers, teachers, and recordkeepers called scribes.

The lowest part of society was the working class. More than 80 percent of the population belonged to the working class. Peasant men worked on farms and in quarries and mines. Women served as dancers, maids, or hairdressers.

After the yearly flood, it was the peasants' job to plow, plant, and harvest the fields. Some peasants had animals to pull their plows, but others had to do it themselves. Preparing fields and harvesting crops was backbreaking work. And a portion of every harvest went directly to the pharaoh as taxes.

The Written Word

Be a scribe. More effective is a book than a decorated tombstone … A man is perished, his corpse is dust, all his relatives are come to the ground—(but) it is writing that makes him remembered.

From a writing exercise for apprentices wishing to become scribes.

Some work gangs chipped away in the quarries. Rock from the quarry was used to build the pyramids and other large buildings. Blocks of stone were cut by hand from the quarry floor and walls. These blocks weighed several tons each. The work was slow. The laborers' tools were made from stone or metals such as copper and bronze. Their tools dulled quickly. The soft blades chipped off only very small pieces of rock at a time.

Sometimes workers had to crawl under a stone to free it from the quarry rock. They wiggled into a space only slightly larger than their bodies. Their only light came from a small oil lamp. The workers breathed in stone dust that damaged their lungs. And there was always the danger of being crushed by the huge blocks.

Ships carried the stone blocks up or down the Nile. From the ship, large gangs of men used ropes to drag the blocks to the building site. It was hard, sweaty work under the hot Egyptian sun.

Working in the mines was even worse. Workers lay on their stomachs in tight-fitting tunnels and chipped out gold and gems. There was always the danger of being buried alive in a cave-in.

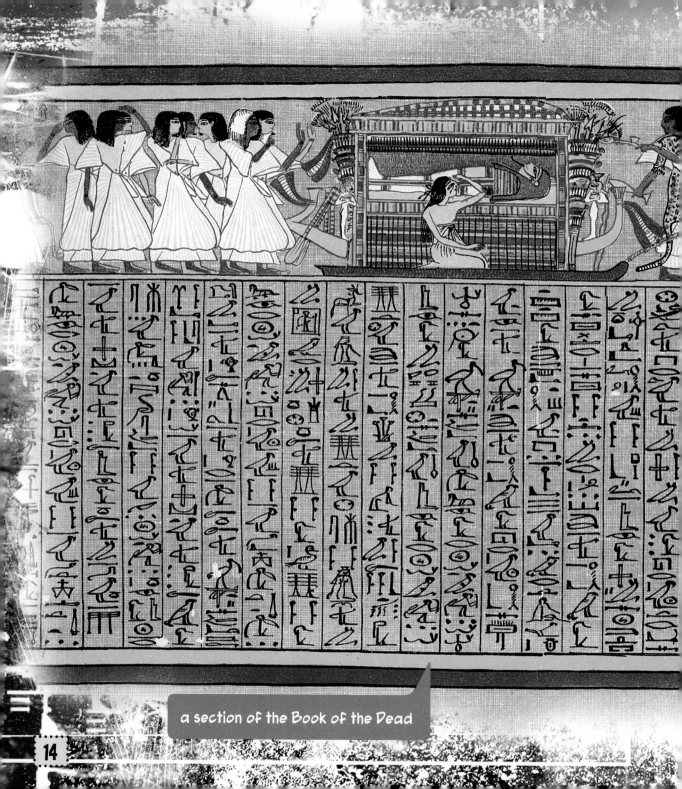

a section of the Book of the Dead

MAKING A MUMMY

For ancient Egyptians, death was a new beginning. Ancient Egyptians believed in the afterlife. People who died met Osiris, the god of the underworld. Those who passed the god's judgment lived forever. The dead were buried with religious texts and magical spells like those found in the Book of the Dead. The spells helped the dead make a successful passage into the afterlife.

The Egyptians believed that the soul of the dead returned to the physical body from time to time. The body could not be left to rot, or the soul might not recognize it.

Special workers preserved the body through a process called mummification. They started by removing the dead person's brain. First a metal hook was pushed up the body's nose and wiggled around to break up the brain. The brain would drain out while the rest of the body dried. Ancient Egyptians didn't know that the brain was important. To them, the heart was the most important internal organ.

Next, they cleaned out the inside of the body. Workers removed the intestines, liver, stomach, and lungs. But they left the heart. Ancient Egyptians believed that the heart was used during the soul's final judgement.

The body was washed with water, then with palm wine. They packed and covered the body with a natural mineral salt called natron. The body was left to dry in the salt for about 40 days. Bodies were placed on slightly slanted tables to allow the fluids to drain.

FOUL FACT

Between the 1400s and 1700s, Europeans used mummies as a cure-all medicine. The bodies were ground into powder or mixed with other ingredients and eaten.

After 40 days, the natron was removed. The body was much lighter. Packing was sometimes stuffed inside the body to make it appear fuller and more lifelike. Finally, the body was washed with perfumed oils and wrapped with linen bandages. Amulets for protection were placed in the wrappings.

The mummy was then placed in a tomb. During the Old Kingdom, pharaohs' tombs were pyramids. The largest pyramids were at Giza. Later pharaohs preferred hidden underground tombs. Many of these tombs were in the Valley of the Kings.

Coffins were decorated to look like the person who had died.

BREAD AND BAD TEETH

Both rich and poor Egyptians ate a lot of bread. But theirs didn't come presliced from the grocery store. And it could be crunchy! Eating bread in ancient Egypt might mean losing a tooth.

Grain, such as wheat and barley, was the main food product of ancient Egyptian farms. The farms grew so much grain that bread and porridge were the main meals of farmers and laborers. Workers were often paid in grain or loaves of bread.

Bread was made into many different shapes. Sometimes the dough was shaped into tall cones. Other times, the dough was made into flat disks. Loaves shaped like fish or people have also been found.

Ancient Egyptians liked variety. They flavored their bread with spices or honey. Ingredients like dates, eggs, butter, and oil added some variety to the bread as well.

BREAD, CIRCA 1500 BC

Grinding flour and making beer was hard, sticky work. Flies were attracted to the sweaty bodies and sweet beer.

Egyptian bread gave a new meaning to whole grain. Sand from the Sahara desert was everywhere. The sand ended up mixed into the bread flour. The gritty sand was rough on the teeth. Over the years, the sand wore the teeth down and exposed the nerves. People with damaged teeth found eating and drinking difficult and painful.

Ancient Egyptians also ate a lot of fruit and vegetables. The rich soil by the Nile River made it easy for farmers to grow plenty to eat. Onions and garlic were particular favorites. Meals were washed down with beer and sometimes wine.

Fish and birds that lived in and near the Nile were also part of the standard diet. Other meats were expensive and eaten mostly by the rich. Ancient Egyptians had no way of refrigerating meat. They had to eat fresh meat quickly or it would spoil. They sometimes preserved meat by drying, smoking, or salting it.

No part of the animal went to waste. People ate the ears, brains, hooves, and guts. The blood was then boiled and used as a seasoning. Blood was sometimes left to thicken, roasted, and eaten as a pudding.

ONIONS

Farmers harvested their crops between March and May.

KEEPING CLEAN

Ancient Egyptians led short lives compared to people today. Many Egyptians died before they reached age 40. Illness was common. Many women died in childbirth. Injuries also made life risky. Even a small cut or a case of diarrhea could be deadly.

People in ancient Egypt didn't know about sanitation. Poor disposal of garbage and bodily waste caused most problems. Garbage piled up outside houses and in alleys. Flies and other disease-carrying creatures flocked to these areas. The ancient Egyptians did not have sewer systems to carry away waste. Instead they tossed their waste into the Nile and its canals. They used this same water for drinking and bathing.

Do you smell that? Then it's time for a bath. Egyptians bathed often, but they did not have soap. Instead, they used natron, the same stuff that was used on mummies.

The rich had bathing areas in their houses. The homes of the rich had as many as 10 rooms, so they had space to put in a bathroom. They bathed in bathrooms with tiled floors and painted walls. But poor people only had one-room houses made of mud bricks. They bathed in canal or river water.

Bathing in the Nile was dangerous and not just because of crocodiles. Tiny pests were always present. People who worked near the water, such as fishermen or brick-makers, were especially at risk to the creepy-crawlies. For example, a creature called the guinea worm entered the human body. It lived under the skin and could grow as long as 3 feet (0.9 m). It caused painful blisters and infection.

Early Egyptians used a system of weights and poles to get water from the Nile safely.

Lice were also a problem. Lice can carry disease. They lay their eggs in human hair. Men and women shaved their heads and bodies to rid themselves of lice.

Of course, this doesn't mean that the ancient Egyptians didn't care about hair. In fact, a head of thick, black hair was seen as a sign of youth. Like today, women with thinning hair got hair extensions, wigs, or tried various recipes to cure baldness. Some recipes included ingredients such as ox blood or donkey liver.

Rich people wore wigs to replace their missing head hair. The wigs were made of human hair, sheep's wool, or plant fibers.

Got something in your eye? The constantly blowing sand, glaring sun, and swarms of flies caused many eye infections. There were many blind and near-blind people.

The desert sand did more than hurt the eyes. People breathed the sand in, causing lung infections and other breathing problems.

FOUL FACT

One recipe for hair tonic called for mixing fats from animals like lions, snakes, and hippos. The mixture was then rubbed into the scalp.

Some wigs contained jewelry, flowers, and gold strands.

Need to go to the bathroom? Most Egyptians either relieved themselves outside or into pots. But some rich people had toilets. These toilets had a stone or wooden seat with a hole in it. Below was a pot that sometimes contained sand. Just like a cat with a litter box, the user would cover the waste with sand. Of course, these pots had to be emptied. And their contents went the same place as everything else—into the river.

MEDICAL TREATMENTS

Need a doctor? You've come to the right place. Ancient Egyptians had some of the most advanced medicine of their time. But they still had some methods we would find gross today.

There were no medical schools, so older doctors trained younger doctors. There were many books that described illnesses and injuries in great detail. The books told the reader what to do in each case and whether something was curable or not. With this information, doctors could give medicines, set broken bones, and treat wounds.

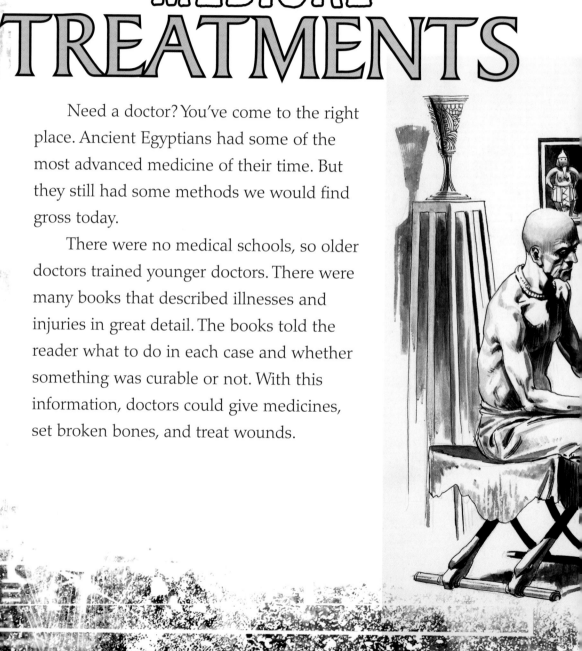

Doctors gave patients medicines made from strange or exotic ingredients.

Many ancient Egyptian cures were practical. For crocodile bites, a doctor sewed up the wound. Many medicines called for honey, which is a natural bacteria killer.

Other treatments depended on odd medicines and practices, and even magic. Some medicines contained animal waste, urine, or blood. One cure called for the patient to sip a special drink made from onion, honey, water, and a mouse's tail. Another remedy called for a mixture of grease and crushed ostrich egg. To try and cure blindness, a doctor would grind up two dry pig's eyes and mix them with honey. He then poured this mixture into the patient's ear.

SOLDIERING FOR THE PHARAOH

For most of its history, ancient Egypt did not have a professional army. In times of war, the pharaoh commanded the army. He drafted men as soldiers. Egyptians dreaded going off to war. Being killed and buried away from their homeland was something they feared.

Most ancient Egyptian troops were known as foot soldiers. They carried spears, axes, and heavy clubs called maces. Long-distance weapons were important too. Archers could attack from a long distance without much danger to themselves. Chariots allowed soldiers to fight without getting tired.

Ancient Egyptian soldiers did not have much protection from enemy weapons. They carried shields, but they were made of leather, not metal. The average soldier did not wear armor or a helmet.

Battle wounds were often nasty. A blow with an ax or a mace could cut or smash through bone. An ax could also cut deep into arms and legs or even take off a limb. Arrows could cut through an eye into the brain. A stone from a sling often crushed a skull or caved-in a chest.

Pharaohs were buried with models of soldiers. The models represented real soldiers and were meant to protect the pharaoh in the afterlife.

Prisoners of War

Slaves in ancient Egypt were often prisoners captured during battles. This ancient text describes prisoners of war in Egypt during the reign of Ramses III.

I gave to them captains of archers, and chief men of the tribes, branded and made into slaves, impressed with my name; their wives and their children were made likewise.

Papyrus Harris, New Kingdom

DOING TIME

Thinking of breaking the law? Think again. The ancient Egyptians did not have a set of written laws. Instead pharaohs were in charge. Their word was law.

Ancient Egypt did have courts. Most trials were held in local courts. Some trials were held before a royal court. The pharaoh or his chief advisor was the judge.

Trials could be harsh affairs. Judges might believe that one side was lying. To get the truth, the judges had these people beaten with sticks.

Ancient Egypt did not have jails. Instead, criminals would have to pay fines or receive harsh punishments. A common punishment was 100 blows with a stick. Ears and noses might be cut off. Sometimes whole families could be punished for the actions of one member.

Murder and treason were punished with death. Execution methods included being burned alive, being run through with a wooden stake, and being eaten by crocodiles.

Tomb raiding was the worst crime in ancient Egypt. Punishment was death by torture.

The royal court tried cases involving the death penalty.

Illness, injury, and hard work were only a few things that shaped how ancient Egyptians lived. They had a lot to worry about, both in this life and the next!

CHAPTER TWO

THE BLOODY, ROTTEN

ROMAN EMPIRE

ROME
753 BC–AD 476

PAGE 44

LEGEND

— RIVERS
▭ ROMAN EMPIRE
☆ CAPITAL CITY
● CITY
∧ MOUNT VESUVIUS

0 — 200 MI.
0 — 322 KM

N
W — E
S

753 BC
Rome is founded.

509 BC
Rome is now a Republic and citizens elect their leaders.

450 BC
Romans write down their laws for the first time in the Laws of the Twelve Tables.

312 BC
Rome builds its first major road.

THE SENATE

The Roman Senate was the empire's governing body. Senators made important decisions about the Roman empire. These decisions included declaring war, managing funds for public use, and meeting with ambassadors from all over the empire. At various times, there were between 300 and 900 senators.

146 BC
Rome defeats its major rival, the city of Carthage. The Romans tear down every building in Carthage.

27 BC
The civil wars end the Republic. Augustus Caesar becomes the first emperor of the Roman Empire.

47 BC
Julius Caesar becomes dictator of Rome.

44 BC
Political rivals kill Caesar; Civil wars begin.

AD 64
A fire destroys much of Rome.

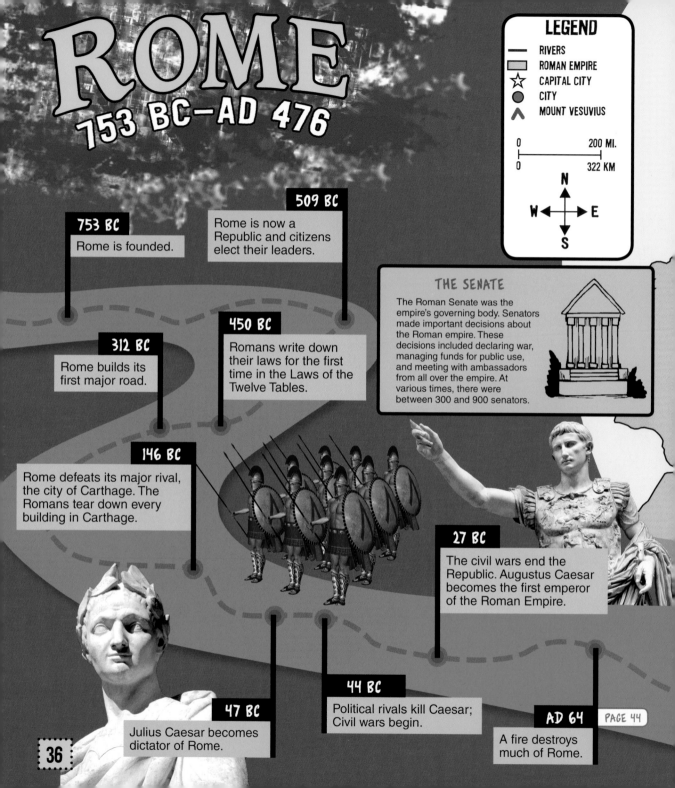

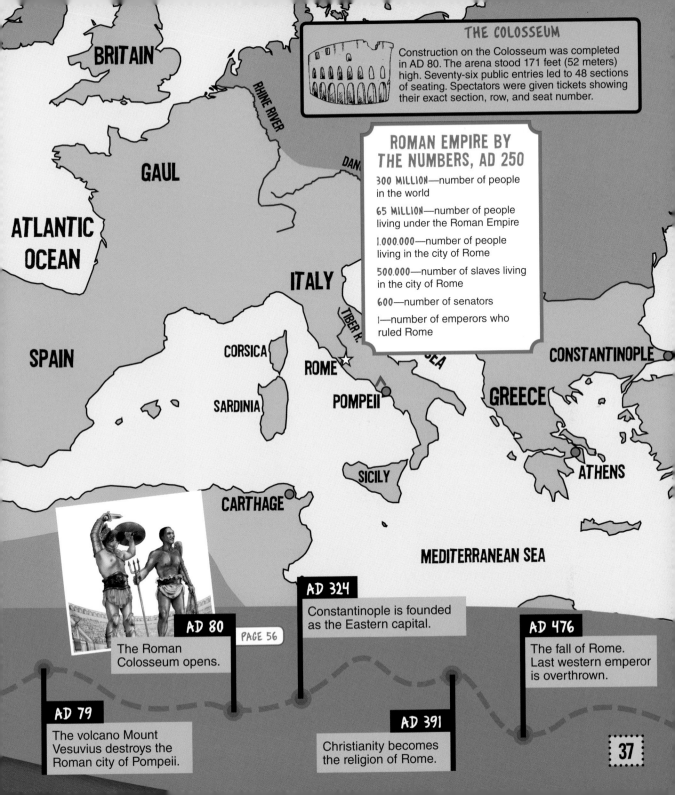

THE COLOSSEUM

Construction on the Colosseum was completed in AD 80. The arena stood 171 feet (52 meters) high. Seventy-six public entries led to 48 sections of seating. Spectators were given tickets showing their exact section, row, and seat number.

BRITAIN

RHINE RIVER

GAUL

DANU

ATLANTIC OCEAN

ITALY

SPAIN

CORSICA

ROME

TIBER R.

CONSTANTINOPLE

SARDINIA

POMPEII

GREECE

ROMAN EMPIRE BY THE NUMBERS, AD 250

300 MILLION—number of people in the world

65 MILLION—number of people living under the Roman Empire

1,000,000—number of people living in the city of Rome

500,000—number of slaves living in the city of Rome

600—number of senators

1—number of emperors who ruled Rome

SICILY

ATHENS

CARTHAGE

MEDITERRANEAN SEA

AD 324

Constantinople is founded as the Eastern capital.

AD 80

PAGE 56

The Roman Colosseum opens.

AD 476

The fall of Rome. Last western emperor is overthrown.

AD 79

The volcano Mount Vesuvius destroys the Roman city of Pompeii.

AD 391

Christianity becomes the religion of Rome.

FILTHY STREETS

Two thousand years ago, the Roman Empire ruled all the lands that bordered the Mediterranean Sea. The ancient Romans had many tools that helped make their lives easier. But there were also parts of Roman life that were dirty, gross, or even deadly.

The Romans grew rich off their empire. Gold, silver, and other treasures flowed into the city. There were large public buildings and many expensive homes. There was also a sports arena and two racetracks.

But Rome was not all gold and riches. Garbage filled the streets in the poorer parts of the city. There was also plenty of human and animal waste. Only the very rich had running water. Human waste piled up outside apartment buildings. Animals lived on the streets, dropping waste as they moved about.

Shops lined the streets of ancient Rome.

FOUL FACT

People killed their animals on the street. The animal remains were tossed in the sewer.

Rome was a messy place. Citizens produced more than 110,000 pounds (50,000 kg) of solid waste every day.

Rome's sewers emptied into the nearby Tiber River. Rainwater was supposed to wash the waste from the sewers into the river. There were big openings on the street for people to dump waste into the sewers. The holes did nothing to hide the stench coming from them.

Few homes had toilets. Some people paid to use public toilets, which were set up over the sewers. Other people used chamber pots.

By law Romans were supposed to empty the chamber pots into a sewer drain. But some people lived in tall apartment buildings. They did not want to carry smelly pots down the many stairs to the drains. So they just emptied the pots out their windows. People passing by were sometimes showered in waste.

There were laws against throwing bodily fluids out the window. Because there were no streetlights, the laws were impossible to enforce at night.

The garbage and animal waste mixed together on the streets. Everyone walked in this slimy mess. Workers were hired by the city to keep the streets clean. But the sewage would always build up again.

The Tiber River was polluted with garbage and human waste.

CITIZENS AND SLAVES

In Rome there were free people and slaves. Many of the free people were Roman citizens. Other free people included foreigners, merchants, or diplomats.

Although Roman women were citizens, they had fewer rights than men. Women could own property. But they could not vote or hold government offices. Women had male guardians all their lives. The guardians were usually husbands or male relatives.

The wealthiest Roman citizens had power over the poor. Rich Romans bought and sold goods throughout the empire. They even bought and sold people.

Thousands of slaves worked in and around Rome. Slaves were bought and sold at auctions. There they were stripped naked and kept in pens. This way, potential buyers could see for themselves that the slaves were healthy.

Some slaves were treated well. A few were paid, and some gained their freedom. But for most, life as a slave was horrible. Some slaves killed their babies at birth rather than allow them to become slaves.

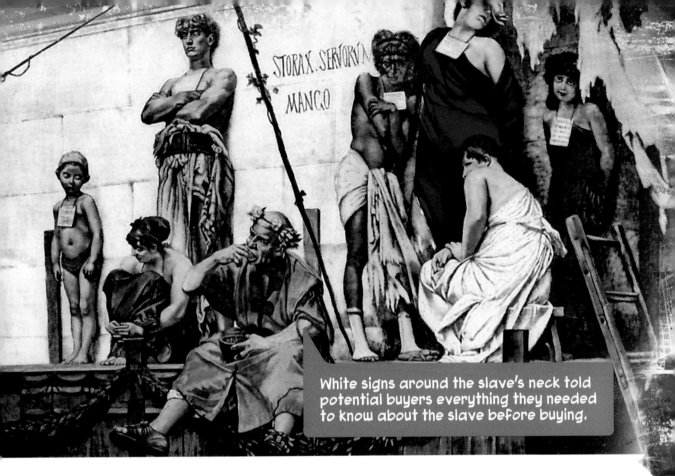

White signs around the slave's neck told potential buyers everything they needed to know about the slave before buying.

Some owners branded or tattooed their slaves' faces. Other slaves were bound with heavy neck chains or collars so they could not escape. Some slaves had to wear tags that showed their masters' names.

There was nothing fair in the treatment of slaves. An owner could beat, torture, or kill a slave for any reason. One Roman broke the legs of a slave who annoyed him. A slave who killed his owner was put to death. But so were all the other slaves in the household—men, women, and children.

In AD 64, a fire swept through Rome. The city's wooden buildings fed the flames that burned for six days and seven nights.

Edenu dicit
Assidus hic
diditur

Many ancient Romans ate their meals at food stands beneath their apartment buildings.

DEADLY HOMES

After a long day at work, imagine coming home to find three people sleeping in your bed! It might seem crowded, but ancient Romans were used to it.

At one time, the city of Rome was home to more than 1 million people. Most Romans lived in apartment buildings above shops. The poorest people shared rooms on the highest stories. Some buildings were eight or nine stories high. These buildings were not safe. The first floor or two might be made of sturdy stone. But the higher stories were often made only of mud and wood. Many buildings fell under their own weight. Those unlucky enough to be in a collapsing building often died.

Apartment buildings also burned down. Although cooking inside the apartments was discouraged, some people did it anyway. Carelessly tended flames from lamps or cooking fires could have a horrible effect. The buildings were built with mud brick and timber that caught on fire easily and burned quickly. There were no fire alarms or fire escapes. People on the highest floors often died.

Building owners rarely cared about these deaths. One owner was actually happy that one of his buildings collapsed. He planned to rebuild and charge higher rents.

Rich Romans ate lying down.

FOUL FACT

Guests at a Roman dinner party might snack on grasshoppers, grubs, or animal parts.

NASTY MEALS

Imagine showing up to a friend's house for dinner. Instead of burgers and fries, you're served snails and pig's stomach! Romans couldn't just go to a restaurant or grocery store to get their meals. Food came from farms all over the empire.

Most Romans ate simple meals. The poorest ate bread or porridge with vegetables. Those with more money sometimes had fish. Few Romans ate meat, which was too expensive.

The wealthy, of course, ate well. They threw fancy dinner parties that lasted for hours. Some Romans went broke trying to impress their friends.

The hosts served strange food. Unusual dishes at these parties included ostrich or peacock. Tongue and brains were eaten along with the meat. Sometimes mice were used as stuffing for birds or other animals. A favorite dish was a small bird called the figpecker. Diners ate all parts of this bird except its beak.

Both rich and poor Romans used olive oil for cooking and flavoring. But even more popular was garum. This sauce was made from aged fish heads, fins, and guts. It was poured over most foods and even used as a medicine.

GRASSHOPPERS

KEEPING CLEAN

Bath time! It's time to climb into the tub—with 1,500 other people. Being clean was important to Romans. Many people bathed daily at public bathhouses. They sat in warm pools or steam rooms. While soaking, people visited and did business. Men and women bathed at different times.

There were hot baths and cold baths. Slaves heated the baths beneath the floor with wood fires. Aqueducts brought in 198,130 gallons (750,000 liters) of fresh spring water a day.

Romans did not have soap. Instead, they rubbed themselves with olive oil. Then they scraped themselves clean with a curved metal tool. The oil helped remove dirt.

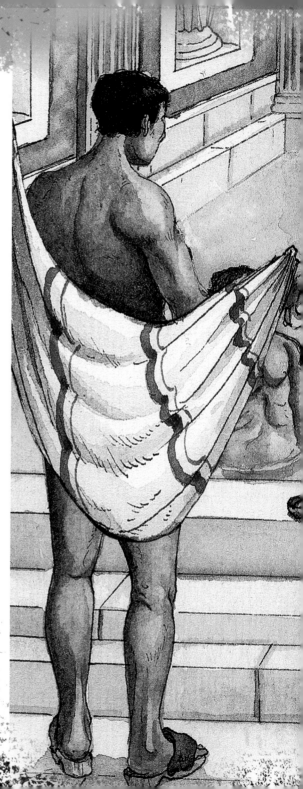

Without soap, Romans had to find other ways to clean their clothes. They made up a cleaner that used human urine. It worked. To collect the pee, laundry workers set out pots on the street. Roman men would relieve themselves into these pots. The dirty clothes were soaked and scrubbed in vats of urine.

The baths and laundries did not keep the Romans safe from fleas and lice. Dirty streets and homes helped keep the number of pests high. Romans had no way to rid themselves of these annoying creatures. People tried getting rid of the pesky bugs by rubbing themselves with dog fat or drinking a concoction that included bits of dead skin.

FOUL FACT

The emperors Nero and Vespasian put a tax on urine. The urine was collected from pots and then sold, usually to laundries or leather shops.

DISEASE AND DOCTORS

Romans were in constant danger from sickness and infection. Roman doctors, who did not understand what caused disease, could do little to stop outbreaks. Many people caught malaria. Sometimes people got smallpox. Thousands became sick and died every year. Only 50 percent of children survived to become adults.

Got a headache? Drink some goat dung soup. That was just one of the many odd medicines Romans used. Roman doctors had a wide variety of medicines, mainly herbs. But there were many treatments that did not work. Romans routinely took pills made from dried bugs or crushed-up snakes. Swellings were packed with animal waste.

Many doctors were self-taught. In fact, any man with some tools and herbs could claim he was a doctor. While there were a number of good doctors, there were also many frauds. Poor Romans did not have the luxury to be picky about who treated them.

Special doctors cared for gladiators and made sure they stayed healthy and fit.

Pain and the Doctor

Now a surgeon should be youthful ... with a strong and steady hand which never trembles ... with vision sharp and clear, and spirit undaunted; filled with pity, so that he wishes to cure his patient, yet is not moved by his cries, to go too fast, or cut less than is necessary; but he does everything just as if the cries of pain cause him no emotion.

Aulus Cornelius Celsus
Doctor and author of De Medicina

Certain animals were sacrificed to each god. Bulls, rams, and boars were acceptable gifts for gods.

BLOODY SACRIFICES

The Romans worshipped many gods and goddesses. Popular gods were Jupiter and his wife, Juno. Mars and Venus also had many followers. Rulers often claimed gods or goddesses as their ancestors.

Romans made sacrifices to important gods. It was hoped that the gods would be pleased with the gifts. The most common sacrifice was a goat or a cow. A priest would kill the animal and would search the liver for messages from the gods. Then he burned the liver, fat, guts, and bones on the god's altar. After the ceremony, the Romans cooked and ate the rest of the animal. Roman families had their own household gods. These gods protected the family from harm. They were given gifts of grain or wine and received part of a family's meal.

Romans held many official religious events throughout the year. In the middle of February, priests sacrificed several goats and a dog to the god Pan. This celebration was held to represent the founding of Rome. In October Romans would hold the October Horse, a chariot race held in honor of the god Mars. A priest killed one of the winning horses and cut off its head. Two teams fought over the head, which was thought to bring good luck.

CRIME AND PUNISHMENT

Romans who broke the law could end up losing their lives. There were many kinds of punishments, but jail time was not one of them. The Romans used prisons only to hold prisoners before their trial or punishment.

Citizens could not be given physical punishment for minor crimes like forgery or lying. Instead, guilty citizens might have to pay a fine or leave Rome. Sometimes they were sent to live alone on small islands. Those who committed major crimes, like treason or murder, might have their heads cut off. Others could be thrown from a cliff known as the Tarpeian Rock.

Noncitizens faced harsher punishments, like being whipped. The Roman whip had three strands of leather. Each strand was braided with lead balls or sharp pieces of metal. It was sometimes used to beat a criminal to death.

Hanging from a cross was considered the most disgraceful way to die.

Death was the penalty for crimes like treason, murder, stealing, and arson. Arsonists were burned alive. But one of the worst forms of death was being tied or nailed to a wooden cross. The victim often died slowly and painfully. Only foreigners and slaves could be whipped to death, burned alive, or hung on a cross.

People who committed crimes against Rome were thrown off Tarpeian Rock.

DEADLY SPORTS

Romans enjoyed deadly sports. Competitors took the field knowing they might not leave alive. Emperors and other rich citizens paid to organize the games. Arenas like the Colosseum attracted audiences from all around Rome. More than 50,000 people packed the Colosseum to watch these deadly contests.

Most gladiators were either slaves or prisoners of war. But a few were citizens who fought for respect. Just like today's pro athletes, successful gladiators received star treatment. Women saw them as extremely attractive. Declarations of love were scribbled on walls of the gladiator schools.

Gladiators experienced tough training at special schools. Fighters pledged to endure humiliation and death without protest. But for some, gladiator school seemed like a good choice. They were fed three meals a day, received medical care, and had the chance for fame and money. If they survived long enough, they could even win their freedom.

FOUL FACT

The bodies of people and smaller animals killed at the Colosseum were often dumped into the Tiber River.

Gladiators were expected to die with honor.

At the arena, wild animals battled each other or armed men in the morning. Planners of the games traveled far and wide to find wild animals for the Colosseum. Creatures like rhinos and bears were brought in from great distances. Many animals were killed this way.

In the afternoon, men condemned to death were brought in to fight. Sometimes they were pitted against each other. Other times they battled trained gladiators. The criminals rarely won. The winner's prize was to keep fighting until someone killed him.

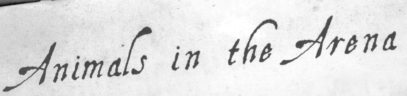

A hunting show organized by the general Pompey had 20 elephants, 600 lions, and more than 400 leopards.

Animals in the Arena

Three times I held gladiator games in my own name and five times in the name of my sons or grandsons. During the games, around 10,000 men fought each other to the death … Twenty-six times I presented the people with hunting shows with wild animals from Africa … and in them around 3,500 animals were killed.

Emperor Augustus (27 BC–AD 14)
From The Deeds of the Divine Augustus

Deaths were common at the Circus Maxiumus.

Romans took their bloody games to the racetrack too. There were several racetracks throughout Rome. The Circus Maximus was the most popular track. It could seat 100,000 fans. Chariots pulled by four horses were crowd favorites.

Horses tore around the track at full speed. They ran all-out for seven laps, or 5 miles (8 km). There were sharp turns at the corners and frequent crashes. Drivers were sometimes dragged to their deaths. They could also be crushed under hooves or wheels.

BATTLE WOUNDS

Soldiers in the Roman army had a rough life. It was the army's job to protect Rome from attack. There was no room for failure, and punishments were harsh. New army recruits and the weakest soldiers were placed at the frontline during battles. This position helped them gain more experience. It also prevented them from running away in fear.

Battle wounds were nasty. The soldiers fought with swords and spears. They also carried large shields. Both Roman and enemy weapons sliced deep into arms and legs. A strong blow from a sword could split a soldier's head open. Spear thrusts could cause fatal wounds.

Roman military training was tough. Beating with thick sticks was a common punishment. Sometimes a commanding officer ordered a soldier beaten to death. Occasionally the soldier's head was cut off afterward. Deserters were usually nailed to a cross. When large groups of soldiers deserted, the punishment was harsh. The commanding officer selected every 10th man. The other soldiers then beat the selected men until they died.

Whether you were a soldier, gladiator, slave, or citizen, life was dirty, disgusting, and deadly in ancient Rome!

Roman soldiers fought their enemies at close range.

CHAPTER THREE

THE HORRIBLE, MISERABLE MIDDLE AGES

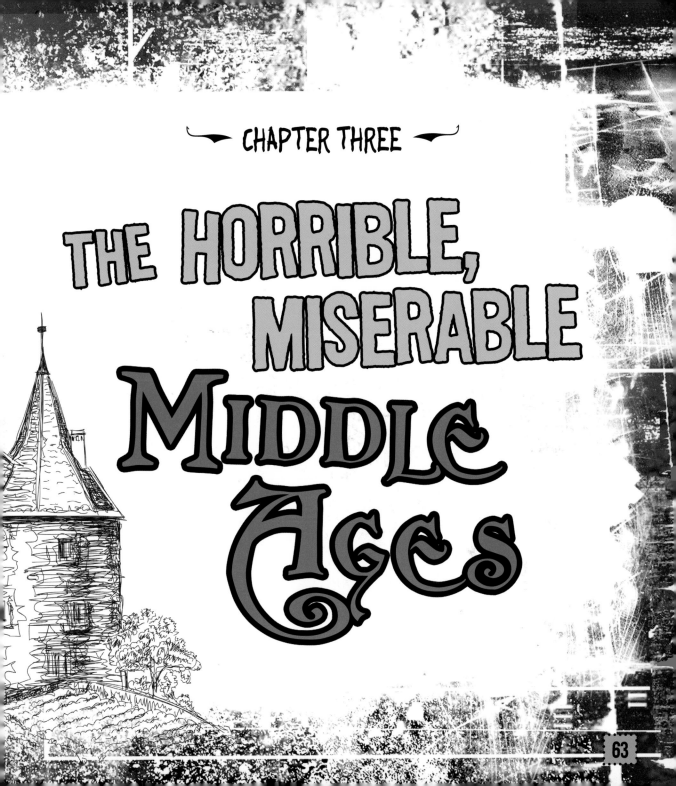

EUROPE DURING THE MIDDLE AGES
AD 476–1400

AD 476 PAGE 66

The last Roman emperor in the West is removed from power. Some historians use this date to mark the beginning of the Middle Ages.

AD 800 PAGE 66

Cities are in decline. Most people live in the country on manors owned by lords.

AD 1000

Armed horseman called knights serve their lords in battle. They become a symbol of the Middle Ages.

MEDIEVAL SOCIAL ORDER
–ALSO CALLED THE FEUDAL SYSTEM–

KING

NOBLES

KNIGHTS

PEASANTS AND SERFS

AROUND AD 800

New farming techniques are invented that allow medieval farmers to grow more food.

PAGE 80

AROUND AD 1050

Medieval people start to live in towns for the first time since the Roman Empire collapsed.

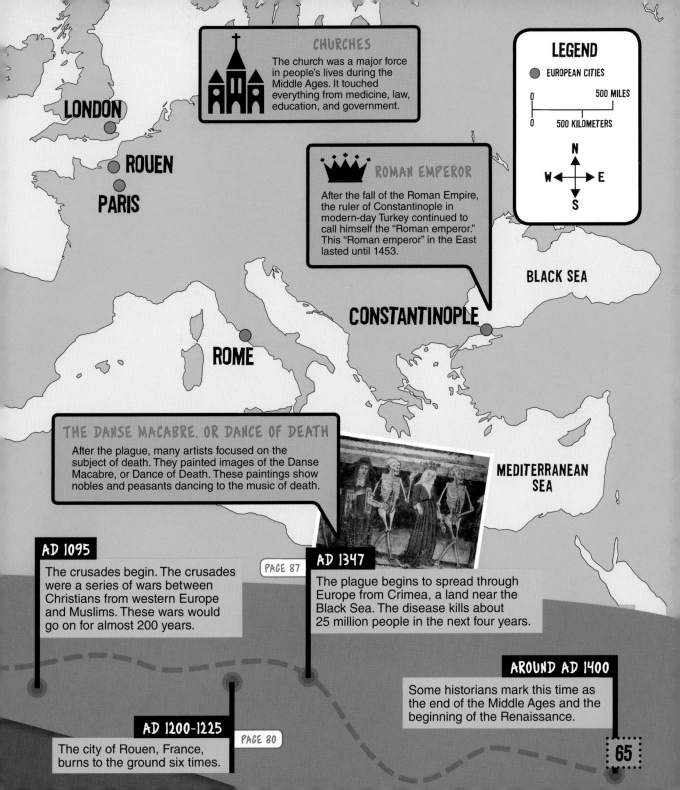

CHURCHES

The church was a major force in people's lives during the Middle Ages. It touched everything from medicine, law, education, and government.

LONDON

ROUEN

PARIS

ROMAN EMPEROR

After the fall of the Roman Empire, the ruler of Constantinople in modern-day Turkey continued to call himself the "Roman emperor." This "Roman emperor" in the East lasted until 1453.

LEGEND

● EUROPEAN CITIES

0   500 MILES

0   500 KILOMETERS

N
W   E
S

BLACK SEA

CONSTANTINOPLE

ROME

THE DANSE MACABRE, OR DANCE OF DEATH

After the plague, many artists focused on the subject of death. They painted images of the Danse Macabre, or Dance of Death. These paintings show nobles and peasants dancing to the music of death.

MEDITERRANEAN SEA

AD 1095

The crusades begin. The crusades were a series of wars between Christians from western Europe and Muslims. These wars would go on for almost 200 years.

PAGE 87

AD 1347

The plague begins to spread through Europe from Crimea, a land near the Black Sea. The disease kills about 25 million people in the next four years.

AROUND AD 1400

Some historians mark this time as the end of the Middle Ages and the beginning of the Renaissance.

AD 1200-1225

PAGE 80

The city of Rouen, France, burns to the ground six times.

DIRTY WORK

In 476 AD the fall of the Roman Empire in the west gave way to the Middle Ages. Some things in the Middle Ages were great. But other things were filthy!

During this time Europe was broken into manors run by lords. Serfs were bound to manors and paid money to manor lords. Serfs worked the land from dawn to dusk.

Nobles didn't control peasants, but that didn't make their lives easier. Peasants farmed the land under a blazing sun and in driving rain. And by the end of the day, they smelled. With no running water, there was no easy way to wash off the filth. Most peasants bathed once a week at most. They bathed in water from nearby streams where they also dumped sewage and trash.

The water used for laundry was just as nasty. Peasants wore the same stiff, itchy clothes day in and day out. Some wool clothing was never washed but simply brushed.

Peasants did what they could to stay clean. They washed their hands several times a day. After meals, they paired with a friend or family member to pick off lice crawling on their clothes.

FOUL FACT

Monks filled tanks with rainwater for bathing and drinking. This water was pretty clean as long as birds didn't fall in.

Serfs and peasants worked long hours in fields.

ROTTING TEETH

The only things that smelled worse than peasants' clothing in the Middle Ages were their dirty, rotting teeth. People didn't use toothbrushes or toothpaste. Many chewed herbs to cover their smelly breath. They also rinsed with vinegar and wine to clean their mouths.

Bad breath was the least of their dental worries. Treatments for cavities and rotted teeth were few. Some people wrongly believed worms caused cavities. They placed an open flame under their jaw to force "worms" out of their gums. Others turned to a tooth-puller, who was often also a barber. These untrained doctors yanked teeth from the gums with a pair of pliers.

Trained doctors would not pull teeth because the patient could die from bleeding. Rich patients who survived this treatment replaced their pulled teeth with fake ones made of cow bone. Most people, however, were left gumming their stale bread.

A Proven Remedy

Take some newts, by some called lizards, and those nasty beetles which are found in fens [marshes] during the summer time, calcine [heat] them in an iron pot and make a powder thereof.

Wet the forefinger of the right hand, insert it in the powder, and apply it to the tooth frequently, refraining from spitting it off, when the tooth will fall away without pain. It is proven.

From a 13th-century guide to curing a toothache (Not to be tried at home!)

Families gutted animals and prepared food in their homes.

TRENCHERS AND OTHER TREATS

Dry bread and a lack of vitamins left commoners with loose teeth and spongy gums. People suffered from scurvy and other illnesses because their meals changed little from day-to-day. Most people filled up on bread, beer, and a mushy porridge made from vegetables and grains. Without refrigerators, fruits and vegetables could not be chilled and shipped. People ate only what was in season and available.

Meat was too expensive for most commoners. Peasants ate whatever they could catch, including rabbits, wild beavers, and pigeons. Peasants and nobles alike could not afford to let valuable meat spoil. They often dried meat to keep it from rotting. Then they boiled it back into chunks that were easy to chew. To make this meat mush taste better, they used many spices. Meat was also stored covered in a gel made from boiled cow hooves.

With so few foods available, nothing could be wasted. Chefs of the nobles cooked up animal brains, lungs, and stomachs. The rich feasted on such delights as bear paws, boar guts, and other organ meat.

Cooks were creative. Surprise dishes, such as a goose hidden inside a peacock, would delight the nobles and their guests. Also pleasing were meals made of animal pairs. Chefs would serve the front end of a rooster attached to a baby pig's back end.

Meat was sometimes eaten on trenchers. These stale pieces of bread soaked up grease and juices. When the lords were done eating, they gave the trenchers to peasants. For peasants, these soaked, stale pieces of bread were a real treat!

FOUL FACT

Diners at nobles' feasts used their best manners. They remembered not to fart or pick flea bites at the table.

Nobles feasted on large meals that were often shared with pets. Any leftovers were given to peasants.

FOUL FACT

People in the Middle Ages didn't have toilet paper. Instead, they used lace, wool, hay, leaves, and even seashells.

MEDIEVAL CASTLE BATHROOM

NO FLUSHING

The food in the Middle Ages left many doubled over and running for the nearest bathroom. It's a good thing many homes had indoor toilets. But people didn't want to spend a lot of time in medieval bathrooms. Waste wasn't flushed away. Instead, a simple wooden toilet connected to a small pipe. The pipe carried waste away — but not too far. The waste pooled in a hole behind the house called a cesspit. This pit was lined with timber or stone so it wouldn't leak to other areas.

In England the men who cleaned out cesspits were called gong farmers. These workers filled tubs with waste and emptied them farther from town. Gong farmers were hardworking, unpopular people. Covered with smelly waste, they lived only with each other. Some died from breathing the fumes or, worse, falling into the pits.

Townspeople without indoor toilets used outhouses or chamber pots. An outhouse was a shack with a bench. A hole in the bench led to a waste-filled pit below. Those without an outhouse used chamber pots. They sometimes dumped these pots out the window onto the street below. This practice didn't happen often, as people could be fined for adding to the town's filth.

Some people built their homes above a stream so their bathroom could empty into it. People often said "bridges are for wise men to go over, and fools to go under." Fools also used public bathrooms. These dirty bathrooms had wooden floors and weren't always safe. Records show that some people fell through bathroom floors into the filth below. The smart ones knew to hold it until they got home.

CHAMBER POT

In the Middle Ages, it was against the law to toss waste into the street and onto others.

FOUL FACT

John the Fearless had a padded toilet seat. The Duke's poop dropped into a stone pit. People can still see it today—the pit that is, not the poop.

COLD CASTLES

Nobles lived in huge stone castles or large homes called manors. While the homes looked beautiful from the outside, inside they could be cold and dark.

Fireplaces were the main source of heat for castles. But this warmth was usually reserved for the lord and his family, especially at night. Servants and workers sometimes slept on cold stone floors. Their only heat came from oven fires.

Bathrooms in castles often had no windows to let out the smell of human waste. Bathrooms were sometimes built sticking out from the walls of castle towers. Waste from these bathrooms fell on whatever—or whomever—was below.

Most castles were built as military sites and often came under attack. Capturing a castle wasn't an easy task. Attackers often waded through wide moats filled with dirty water, underwater spikes, and human and animal waste. Others crawled through filthy bathroom shafts to enter the building!

Medieval castles looked beautiful, but they were cold, smelly places.

MEDIEVAL TOWNS

By AD 1050 rows of small houses cropped up in towns across Europe. Peasants often lived in cramped one-room houses. Animals, including cows, would often share the same room with family members.

Later houses were two-stories. They had a shop on the main floor and living space on the top. Homes were built close together and often made of wood and straw. Indoor fires cooked food and provided heat, but they also burned people and homes. The city of Rouen, France, burned down six times in 25 years.

If things were somewhat smelly inside homes, they were even worse in city streets. Animals were often gutted at market. Their insides were thrown onto the street. Blood and guts flowed through a gutter in the middle of streets made of hard-packed dirt. Wider streets had gutters on each side to collect animal waste. Men called rakers piled trash into carts and dumped it downwind from town.

Medieval towns were filled with shops, waste, and smells.

People were fined for polluting the town with animal guts. Towns also tried to stop the smelly practice of selling spoiled meat. Anyone caught selling rotten food would have their goods burned as punishment. They were also forced to sit very close to the fire, breathing the smell of burning spoiled meat. It's no wonder people held flowers on their way through town to fight the smell of everyday life.

BARBER-SURGEONS

From town to country, people in medieval times led lives marked by illness and injury. Hard work, animal bites, and battle wounds left many in need of doctors. There were medical schools but few doctors to be found. Only the rich could afford a trained doctor. Even these professionals sometimes used odd medicines such as ground-up earthworms.

Those who could not afford doctors relied on folk medicine and common healers to cure them. Patients swallowed herbs or chanted to cure sickness. At best, these folk cures did no harm. At worst, they killed the patient. Some treatments were more gross than deadly, such as putting pig poop on a bleeding nose. Some animal dung treatments actually worked, but you won't find them used at a doctor's office today.

Few medieval doctors had formal training. Many tried odd treatments to cure patients.

For bigger health problems, those who could not find a doctor went to the next best thing—a barber-surgeon. Barber-surgeons performed a common operation called bloodletting. The same knives and razors used for haircuts came in handy for this treatment. For this operation, a barber made a small cut in the vein of a patient and let the blood pool in a dish. The barber then studied the blood for clues as to what was making the person sick. Barbers studied blood by smelling it, touching it, and even tasting it. Barber-surgeons also tested urine by tasting it.

Most surgeries of the time were simple. The most serious operations were for those wounded in battle. Even for amputations, surgeons didn't have very good medicines. Lucky patients would pass out at the first cut of a crude saw. Other patients breathed chemicals on a soaked rag, which could also kill them.

MEDIEVAL BLOODLETTING KNIFE

People believed that bloodletting would rid them of disease.

FOUL FACT

Medieval doctors also used leeches to suck blood from patients. Some doctors still use leeches today!

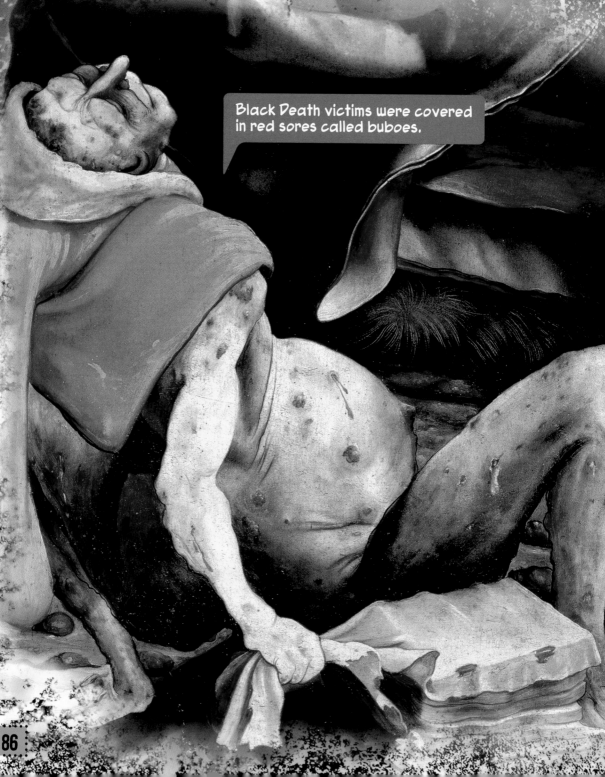

PLAGUE HORRORS

Doctors and barber-surgeons were not ready for the plague that swept through Europe starting in the mid-1300s. The plague, called Black Death, killed nearly one-third of the people in Europe. People caught the plague from fleas that had feasted on wild rats. Once the plague showed its signs, it could kill within one week. Panic swept through towns and villages. Even doctors ran in fear from patients with signs of the plague.

The first symptom was usually a small, black bump where a diseased flea had bitten the person. Larger bumps, called buboes, soon followed. Buboes were often found in the neck, armpits, or groin area. These bumps could be as small as an egg or as large as an apple. Next, dark spots of blood seeping beneath the skin spread throughout the body. By this time, little could be done to save the patient. The total number of dead was too much for even the biggest towns to handle.

Bodies were left outside homes to be picked up by passing workers. These workers were often released prisoners. They were the only ones willing to do the dirty job of collecting dead bodies. Mass graves filled quickly. Some bodies were dumped into the sea. Other bodies were left to lie in the street.

Adding to the horror were patients gone mad with disease and fright. Some would dance on the rooftops, while others dug their own graves. Leaving piles of dead, the plague was a most disgusting time in the Middle Ages.

FOUL FACT

Some people used plague victims when trying to capture a castle. They tossed plague-infected bodies over the castle walls as weapons.

A Pitiful Sight

In a book called The Decameron, written in the 1350s, Giovanni Boccaccio describes the disgusting sights and smells of the plague:

The plight of the lower and most of the middle classes was even more pitiful to behold. Most of them remained in their houses, either through poverty or in hopes of safety, and fell sick by thousands. Since they received no care and attention, almost all of them died. Many ended their lives in the streets both at night and during the day; and many others who died in their houses were only known to be dead because the neighbours smelled their decaying bodies. Dead bodies filled every corner.

CHAPTER FOUR

THE ROUGH, STORMY AGE OF VIKINGS

THE ERA OF THE VIKINGS

AD 793–1066

AD 793 | PAGE 94

Vikings raid Lindisfarne in England. This is the first recorded Viking attack.

AD 825

Vikings discover Iceland.

PAGE 98 | **AD 845**

Vikings raid France and establish Dublin, Ireland.

AD 865

Vikings conquer most of central England.

AD 870

Vikings begin settling Iceland.

AD 911

The Viking leader Rollo becomes duke of Normandy in France.

PAGE 108 | **AD 930**

Vikings in Iceland set up the first European parliament.

VINLAND MAP

In 1965 Yale University announced that it had a map that proved Vikings had reached North America before Christopher Columbus. Today experts debate whether the "Vinland Map" is real or fake.

LEGEND

- VIKING HOMELANDS
- VIKING SETTLEMENTS
- • • • • ROUTES

| 0 | 100 MI |
| 0 | 161 KM |

N
W — E
S

NORWAY

SWEDEN

SCOTLAND

NORTH SEA

IRELAND

DENMARK

WALES

ENGLAND

DEADLY JOURNEY

Thorvald Eriksson, Leif's brother, made his own journey to North America. He was attacked and killed by Native Americans in 1004. He became the first European killed and buried in the New World.

GRAVE SHIPS

In 1880 and 1906, two Viking grave ships, *Gokstad* and *Oseberg*, were discovered in Norway.

PAGE 107 AD 1000

Leif Eriksson reaches North America.

AD 985 PAGE 107

Erik the Red successfully reaches Greenland.

PAGE 121 AD 1066

The last Viking invasion takes place; William the Conqueror becomes king of England.

RAIDERS FROM THE SEA

For nearly 300 years, a group known as the Vikings terrorized Europe. These men from Scandinavia attacked anywhere their ships could reach. These "Devil Children" were as nasty as they were tough.

The first major Viking attack took place in AD 793, at the English holy island known as Lindisfarne. From then on, the Vikings looted towns and villages. They destroyed whole communities. They captured thousands of slaves. Nobody escaped the Vikings.

These wolves of the sea would eventually be tamed by time. But before then, they would come to rule large territories across Europe.

A Viking raid was a fearsome thing. Their ships would appear suddenly and without warning. A single ship could carry about 24 heavily armed warriors. Often there was more than one ship in a raid.

The largest Viking ship ever found could carry 100 warriors.

The Vikings were pagans. To them, only the strongest and most powerful were meant to rule. The Vikings showed no pity or mercy. They set buildings on fire. They killed men, women, and children who tried to escape.

Vikings took anything of value. Churches were prime targets. They held great treasures, and the monks who lived there did not fight back. The Vikings killed all the animals. It was easier to take animal skins and dried meat with them when they left.

Victims of the Vikings were usually men. Women and children were taken as slaves.

Small raids continued throughout the Viking age. But over time, the Vikings became more organized. They built large fleets of more than 300 ships. Villagers were terrified when they saw hundreds of Viking ships sailing toward their homes.

Vikings needed money to conduct their raids. They had a number of ways of getting loot. Sometimes churches, towns, and even whole kingdoms agreed to pay protection money. The Vikings took the payments and promised not to attack. It was a good plan. The payments drained the people of their resources, and the Vikings didn't have to lift a finger.

In 845 an army of Vikings, led by Ragnar Lodbrok, sailed up the Seine River. His fleet of 145 ships attacked Paris, France. The French soldiers were captured and executed. Finally the king of France paid the Vikings' price. He paid nearly 6 tons (5.4 metric tons) of silver and gold. Paying the ransom was a mistake. Other Viking groups heard of the rich bribe and came to claim their own.

Vikings also fought among themselves. Vikings from Denmark and Norway fought over land in Ireland. The Viking settlement of Dublin changed hands several times.

Ragnar Lodbrok often attacked on holy days when soldiers would be in church.

The history of the Vikings has been recorded in stories since around the 13th century.

FOUL FACT

One group of Vikings celebrated war victories by having a feast on the battlefield. They set up their cooking fires among the bodies. The fire cooked their food and burned the bodies of their enemies.

ROUGH AND TOUGH BATTLES

What's more scary—knives, swords, or battle-axes? The victims of the Vikings were faced with answering that question. Villagers were often unarmed. The Vikings could easily cut down these defenseless people.

In war, Vikings usually found themselves facing a well-armed enemy. Wounds could be nasty, and sometimes proved fatal. Iron swords sliced at bodies, arms, and legs. Sometimes limbs were cut off. A strong blow from a sword or axe could split a person's head open. A thrown battle-axe could lodge itself in a body.

Vikings wore armor that covered their chests and backs. Most armor was made of toughened leather, which offered protection without a lot of weight. Some Vikings wore chain mail made of linked metal rings. Others wore steel or leather helmets on their heads. Arms and legs were left bare so they could move easier. Most Viking warriors carried a round wooden shield.

CHAIN MAIL

Warriors called berserkers were especially feared. Some Viking leaders kept these warriors in their armies. The berserkers fought without fear of death. They worked themselves into a wild frenzy called a Berserk Rage. Their only desire during this rage was to kill.

Berserkers did not wear armor or helmets. Instead, they covered their bodies in animal skins. Berserkers were hard to stop even when badly or fatally wounded. In their fury, it was said that they didn't feel any pain.

The existence of berserkers was first recorded in the ninth century.

Berserkers

They advanced without mail-coats, and were as frenzied as dogs or wolves; they bit their shields; they were as strong as bears or boars; they struck men down, but neither fire nor steel could mark them. This was called the Berserk Rage.

From a history of the kings of Norway, written by Icelandic historian Snorri Sturluson.

FIERCE ADVENTURES

Vikings did more than raid and loot. They also traded in foreign lands. They explored the Atlantic Ocean. And they settled distant shores. Above all, Vikings sought adventure.

Viking ships were vessels for adventure. Their wooden boats, called longships, were engineering marvels. They could be powered by sail or by oar. They were fast, sturdy, and easy to steer. And their design made it possible to sail in as little as 20 inches (51 cm) of water. This ability allowed Vikings to travel across oceans and up rivers. They could easily sail to distant towns and cities and attack.

Vessels sailing across the ocean were fitted with a dragon or serpent head. The head was to frighten away evil spirits and sea monsters. These heads earned Viking boats the name "Dragon Ships."

All Viking ships were made of wood. Only oak was used to build warships.

Travel in a Viking ship was a salty situation. The ships leaked and were often in danger of sinking. Sometimes they did sink. Crews had to spend long hours bailing out water.

Viking ships had no cabins. There was no protection from the weather. Crews were often wet from ocean water thrown by wind and waves. Constantly being hit with seawater was rough on the skin. The irritated skin would break out in sores. The salty water stung and kept the sores from healing.

Viking cargo ships, called knorrs, were higher and wider than longships. They also had cargo decks to store supplies. Knorrs could be crowded and smelly places. Settlers traveling to Viking settlements brought their farm animals aboard. The animals peed and pooped in the ship. There was nowhere to go to escape the smell. There was also no privacy when a passenger had to go to the bathroom.

a Viking trading ship

The food could be as rough as the seas. Nothing was cooked, since the risk of starting a fire on a wooden ship was too great. Tough dried meat was washed down with lukewarm water, ale, or sour milk.

The ships may have been dangerous and uncomfortable. But they were the most advanced and seaworthy ships of their time. They carried Vikings on many adventures. They allowed Vikings to cross the North Atlantic. Vikings settled in Ireland and Greenland. And eventually they reached North America.

VIKING HOMES

Vikings were more than sailors or pirates. Even though they spent so much time at sea, they had to call somewhere home. They had families. They raised animals and grew their own food. They were also members of society.

Viking societies were ruled differently, depending on where they lived. In some societies, the king was in charge. Vikings in Iceland were ruled by a parliament. They did not have a king until 1265.

Below the ruling class were aristocrats. These were chieftains and important landowners. Most Vikings were free commoners. At the bottom of society were the slaves. The slaves were people taken captive during raids. Slave men and women were given the hardest, most grueling jobs. They had no rights and were seen as property.

Viking towns were built near the sea. The houses were close together for protection from enemies.

There were some Viking trading towns. But most Vikings lived in one-room houses on farms. The family, farm tenants, and slaves all slept together in the house. Benches along the wall served as beds. There was no privacy.

The winters in much of the Vikings' world were long and hard. A Viking farmhouse had thick walls made of wood, stone, or dirt. There were no windows. A hole in the roof let out some of the smoke from cooking fires. But the house was dark, smoky, and smelly.

The roofs of Viking houses were built to look like their ships.

the inside of a Viking home

Animals had to be kept indoors when it got dark. Otherwise they might freeze to death during cold winter nights. Large farms had barns for the animals. But for many, the house was the only place to put the animals.

The animals provided warmth in the cold winter. But there was a downside. Farm animals aren't house-trained. Straw was laid out to soak up manure and was removed regularly. Still, with no windows to let in fresh air, the smell of soiled straw remained.

The animals could go to the bathroom inside, but that didn't work for people. Viking houses did not have toilets. People used open pits dug in the ground outside the house. In the hotter months, these pits would fill the air with their foul stench. Swarms of flies would buzz around anyone who came near.

ROTTEN FOOD AND BROKEN BONES

Most Viking families grew and raised much of the food they ate. Barley became bread and porridge. Meat came from pigs, horses, cows, goats, and chickens. The Vikings used all of the animal. Blood sausage was a favorite dish. Cows and goats produced milk. There were also beans, cabbage, and other vegetables. And Vikings caught fish.

Cold winters prevented Vikings from growing food year round. In some northern areas, the growing period was very short. Methods of food preservation included pickling, smoking, drying, and salting.

One way the Vikings preserved food is not used often today. Fermentation prevents bacteria from growing on food. It allows the food to last longer. Today we use fermentation to make vinegar or alcohol.

But the Vikings made more than vinegar. They would bury an entire animal in a pit and leave it until it soured. Shark meat, whale meat and blubber, fish, and butter were only some of the items left in the ground to eat later.

But by the end of a long winter, food was in short supply. People were sometimes half-starved by the time winter ended. They also suffered from illnesses like scurvy.

Vikings ate two meals every day, once at 7 a.m. and again at 7 p.m.

Men who fought after being wounded were seen as the bravest warriors.

Vikings faced other health threats. Even a powerful, berserk Viking couldn't defeat lice or fleas. No amount of sword swinging or axe throwing could give the Vikings a victory. They bathed once a week, but there was no getting rid of these gross bugs. Some pests lived inside the body. Tapeworms were common. These wormy creatures made their homes in the small intestine. They could grow to be 1 foot (30.5 cm) long. Tapeworms also caused disease, infection, and even brain damage.

Vikings did not have doctors. Women were the only healers. They used various plants for medicines. They set broken bones.

Viking women also treated battle wounds. To stop bleeding, they rolled hot iron over the wound. This painful process also prevented infection.

Swords and spears were dangerous and deadly. They could easily pierce a man's body. A warrior with pierced guts was sure to die. The women fed some wounded Vikings a porridge made with onions. If an onion smell came from the wound, then everyone knew the guts had been broken open.

BLOODY JUSTICE

Vikings did not have written laws. Few people could read or write. They also had no police or prisons. But they did have laws. Justice was left in the hands of those who had been wronged.

Most guilty people had to pay a fine to the injured party. Sometimes the convicted person was outlawed. Both fines and outlawing were common punishments for murder.

Someone found guilty of stealing, evil sorcery, or lying faced death. Hanging was the most common punishment. But Vikings also cut off heads or burned people alive.

Some Vikings had a system of justice called a blood feud. A person who believed himself wronged by another did not always seek justice. Instead, he or his relatives would kill a member of the wrongdoer's family. This killing often sparked a series of revenge killings between the two families. These feuds could last for generations.

FOUL FACT

Slaves guilty of murder faced a harsh death. Their hands and feet were cut off. Then they were left to die slowly of starvation, blood loss, and thirst.

Although the Vikings had no written laws, they did have honor.

No Home, No Honor

Deserting during battle was seen as a horrible crime. The character Wiglaf in the poem "Beowulf" strips deserters of their property and honor.

Every one of your kindred will be made to move on, with the rights to his land stripped away, when war-chieftains from afar hear the tale told of your flight from your lord, that deed without glory. Death is better for all noble men, than a life of shame!

GODS OF VIOLENCE

The Vikings believed in many gods. Each god represented a different aspect of life, including war or strength. The chief god was one-eyed Odin. He was often shown riding his eight-legged horse, along with two ravens and two wolves. The goddess Frigg, who represented love and marriage, was Odin's wife. Another important god was Thor. Thor was the god of thunder and lightning. He had a hammer that would always return to him.

Vikings believed giants were the enemies of the gods. The god Loki fought on both sides. Loki had half-giant children. One child was a large snake called the Midgard Serpent. Another was a huge wolf called Fenrir.

Vikings offered the gods both human and animal sacrifices. One group hanged nine of every kind of male creature, including men, as a gift to the gods every nine years. Another group sacrificed 99 people and 99 horses. They also killed a large number of dogs and roosters.

Sacrifices were not limited to the gods. Slaves, horses, and dogs of an important Viking sometimes joined their master in death too.

The Viking age came to an end in England with the rule of William the Conqueror. By this time, other countries had strong leaders who lived in big castles and had large armies. It became harder and harder for the Vikings to go on successful raids. The Viking way of life died out.

Thor was the most popular Viking god.

CHAPTER FIVE

THE DREADFUL, SMELLY COLONIES

THE 13 AMERICAN COLONIES
1607–1776

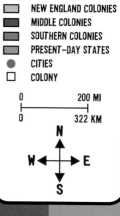

LEGEND

☐	NEW ENGLAND COLONIES
☐	MIDDLE COLONIES
☐	SOUTHERN COLONIES
☐	PRESENT-DAY STATES
●	CITIES
☐	COLONY

0 — 200 MI
0 — 322 KM

N
W ← → E
S

1585

First English colony formed at Roanoke Island; it is deserted sometime before 1600.

1607 PAGE 126

Jamestown and Sagadahoc established; Sagadahoc settlement fails.

PAGE 136

1619

Twenty Africans arrive at Jamestown on a Dutch ship to be sold as servants.

PAGE 129

1620

About 100 colonists arrive on the Mayflower to form Plymouth Colony in Massachusetts.

ESTIMATED POPULATION OF COLONISTS IN AMERICA

	NUMBER OF COLONISTS	LARGEST CITY
1587	120	None
1617	4,000	None
1650	50,400	Boston – 2,000
1700s	275,000	Boston – 7,000
1720s	475,000	Boston – 12,000
1760s	1,500,000	Philadelphia – 19,000
1770s	2,210,000	Philadelphia – 28,000

1664

Maryland passes a law requiring lifelong slavery for Africans brought to the colonies as servants.

WILLIAM BRADFORD ON THE MAYFLOWER'S ARRIVAL IN 1620

"The whole country, full of woods and thickets, represented a wild and savage hue."

From *Of Plymouth Plantation*, 1620-1647

1630

John Winthrop arrives in Massachusetts with 900 Puritans to form Massachusetts Bay Colony with Boston as its headquarters.

PAGE 146

1675-1676

King Philip's War between colonists and American Indians in New England results in the deaths of 600 English colonists and 3,000 American Indians.

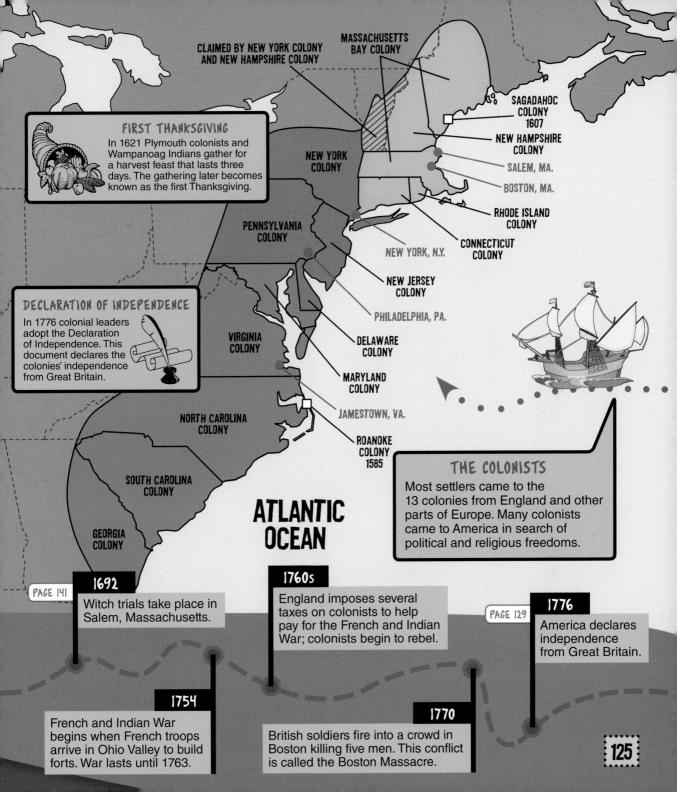

CLAIMED BY NEW YORK COLONY
AND NEW HAMPSHIRE COLONY

MASSACHUSETTS
BAY COLONY

SAGADAHOC
COLONY
1607

NEW HAMPSHIRE
COLONY

SALEM, MA.

BOSTON, MA.

NEW YORK
COLONY

RHODE ISLAND
COLONY

CONNECTICUT
COLONY

NEW YORK, N.Y.

NEW JERSEY
COLONY

PENNSYLVANIA
COLONY

PHILADELPHIA, PA.

DELAWARE
COLONY

VIRGINIA
COLONY

MARYLAND
COLONY

JAMESTOWN, VA.

NORTH CAROLINA
COLONY

ROANOKE
COLONY
1585

SOUTH CAROLINA
COLONY

GEORGIA
COLONY

ATLANTIC
OCEAN

FIRST THANKSGIVING
In 1621 Plymouth colonists and Wampanoag Indians gather for a harvest feast that lasts three days. The gathering later becomes known as the first Thanksgiving.

DECLARATION OF INDEPENDENCE
In 1776 colonial leaders adopt the Declaration of Independence. This document declares the colonies' independence from Great Britain.

THE COLONISTS
Most settlers came to the 13 colonies from England and other parts of Europe. Many colonists came to America in search of political and religious freedoms.

PAGE 141

1692
Witch trials take place in Salem, Massachusetts.

1760s
England imposes several taxes on colonists to help pay for the French and Indian War; colonists begin to rebel.

PAGE 129

1776
America declares independence from Great Britain.

1754
French and Indian War begins when French troops arrive in Ohio Valley to build forts. War lasts until 1763.

1770
British soldiers fire into a crowd in Boston killing five men. This conflict is called the Boston Massacre.

FOUL FACT

In 1610, 175 new settlers arrived at Jamestown, Virginia. They found only 60 of the first 500 colonists alive. Disease and starvation had killed the rest.

When colonists arrived in America, they had to clear land and build shelters.

NEW LAND, NEW HOME

In the 1600s, colonists came to America from Europe with the hopes of freedom and a new beginning. What they found instead was rough land, harsh weather, and dreadful living conditions. When colonists arrived in America, no warm, cozy homes were waiting for them. So they needed to find shelter—fast.

In the southern colonies, the first colonists lived in tents made of sailcloth. They complained bitterly of the bugs. Mosquitoes feasted on the new arrivals.

Other colonists built small wigwams. They tied poles together and covered them with bark and tree branches to keep out the winter's cold. A fire added light, heat, and blinding smoke. In winter, families huddled on the straw floor beneath furs and blankets.

Small shelters offered little protection from the harsh new land.

Some settlers in Massachusetts, New York, and Pennsylvania dug cavelike homes. They lined dirt walls with sticks to prevent the home from collapsing. One wall contained a small door. Bugs skittered in through the tree-branch roof and dropped onto sleepers. Mice, rats, and snakes slithered through the sod.

The first wooden houses were only about 20 feet (6 m) wide by 20 feet (6 m) long. Shutters over the windows kept out the wind, but they also kept out the light. A fire burned constantly to provide light and heat. Everyone ate, worked, and slept in just one room. A lucky family might have a table and one or two chairs. Children stood while they ate their meals. They slept on the floor on mattresses stuffed with rags, cornhusks, or bits of leftover wool. Houses smelled of smoke, stew, and sweaty bodies.

Disease and Death

March 24, 1621 — Plymouth Colony

This month thirteen of our number died. During the last three months, half of those in our colony have perished. Most died from lack of housing. Some suffered from diseases like scurvy, brought on by the long ocean voyage. Of 100 persons, scarcely 50 remain. The living are barely able to bury the dead. There is no one to care for the ill. But spring is coming, and we hope that the deaths will cease and that the sick and lame will recover. All have shown great patience during this time of suffering.

Above quotation is based on the writing of Thomas Prince, as published in The Annals of New England, 1726.

HARDTACK, ANYONE?

Picky eaters didn't last long in the colonies. At first, colonists ate what they brought with them on the ship. They ate dried peas that had to be soaked in water for hours and then boiled. For meat, they had salted pork or beef. When meat became moldy and rotten, colonists scraped away the mold and ate what was left. Their only bread was hardtack, a rock-hard cracker made of flour and water. Beetles called weevils burrowed into the hardtack, which made it easier to eat.

After these supplies ran out, most colonies suffered through a starving time. Some settlers survived on corn that they bought from American Indians. Others tried fishing. The forests were full of wildlife, but most colonists didn't own guns. So they ate whatever they could gather or kill. One Jamestown colonist reported eating "dogs, cats, rats, snakes, toadstools, horsehides, and what not." He was lucky. Many others starved.

HARDTACK

When crops were good, colonists had plenty of food to eat.

In time colonists learned to grow corn. But corn made for a boring diet. In many homes, colonists ate cornmeal mush or porridge for both breakfast and supper. The biggest meal was often a stew of beans, corn, and other vegetables. On a good day, the stew might include raccoon or deer meat. Yum!

NO PRIVACY IN THE PRIVY

Imagine the nice, comfy bathroom you use every day. Now picture a rough tree, dirty pit, or smelly outhouse. Pretty gross, right? But that's what colonists used for bathrooms.

At first, colonists stepped behind a tree or a bush when they needed to go. But as towns grew and people lived closer together, they needed another solution.

Colonists dug pits downhill from their homes and built outhouses or privies over the pit. A board with a hole in the middle formed the seat. Waste fell into the pit. When the pit was full, colonists dug a new pit and moved the outhouse.

People who were very old or sick used a chamber pot. This pottery bowl was dumped outside each morning. Children often did this job. In cities, chamber pots were emptied into the streets, sometimes landing on people passing by.

Animals added to the problem too. Pigs, cows, and horses wandered freely through towns leaving their droppings behind. If colonists didn't watch their steps, they'd carry the stinky mess inside on their shoes.

FOUL FACT

There was no toilet paper in colonial America. Colonists used corncobs to clean themselves. They tossed them in the pit after use.

Most colonial outhouses were small wooden shacks with no windows.

Colonial children worked alongside their parents harvesting crops.

DIRTY JOBS

How would you like to bend over 6,000 times a day planting tiny seeds? Sound like fun? Maybe not to you, but that's how colonists planted their crops.

But before colonists could plant seeds, they had to clear dense forest to make farm fields. Men swung heavy axes to cut down massive trees. Once the huge trees fell, they had to be cut apart and moved. There were no sawmills, so men chopped logs and firewood by hand.

Once the trees were gone, the dirty fieldwork continued. Men, women, and children used hoes and shovels to break up the hard soil. The dirty job got a little easier when plows were invented in the 1670s.

After the fields were plowed, it was time to plant. But that just meant more long hours digging in the dirt. American Indians taught colonists how to plant corn in small hills. Men and women planted corn crops by hand. They used a small stick or their finger to make holes in the dirt for corn seeds.

HARD LABOR

Colonial farms needed workers, as did businesses such as lumber and shipbuilding. Indentured servants and slaves did much of the work. Indentured servants signed contracts promising to work for four to seven years in exchange for a free trip to America.

In 1619 the first African slaves arrived at Jamestown. At first, a few were able to buy their freedom. Later, the laws changed making them slaves permanently. Slaves were considered the owner's property. Trying to escape meant death. Many slaves were beaten, whipped, and worked to death on the farms of colonial America.

Indentured servants and slaves got up at dawn and worked until bedtime. Female servants hauled water, cooked meals, cared for children, and helped in the fields. Male servants cleared land, tended crops, and did whatever else their masters required.

COLONIAL SLAVE AUCTION

Young Slave

When I was nine, I was forced to work even harder. In summer I pounded four bushels of ears of corn every night in a barrel for the chickens. In winter I had to card wool until a very late hour. If I failed at these tasks, I would be harshly punished.

Slave boy in Massachusetts, 1740s

ROUGH ROADS

Getting around the colonies was a chore. The best way to travel was by boat, provided your craft didn't topple over in the churning waters.

Most colonists traveled by foot following old Indian trails through the woods. Trees and bushes barred the way. Travelers jumped or waded across narrow streams. They crossed deep rivers and streams in boats or canoes. Most people couldn't swim.

Carriages and carts were rare. In 1697 Philadelphia had only 30 wheeled vehicles in the entire city. Small, cramped carriages bounced along rough dirt roads. Wheels fell off. Horses got tired. A carriage trip was slow, dusty, and uncomfortable.

Long trips took several days. In remote areas, travelers slept outdoors or stayed with farm families. In towns, they stopped at taverns. The tavern owner provided food, drink, and a shared bed for a price.

In the colonies, people traveled along rough roads to buy or trade goods.

Women were tried and convicted as witches, even though little evidence was presented against them.

WITCH TRIALS

Some colonists blamed witches for bad weather, ill health, dead animals, or failed crops. Women more often than men were labeled witches and put on trial. If a woman was found guilty of being a witch, her punishment was often death. Connecticut held more witch trials than any other colony.

The most famous trials occurred in Salem, Massachusetts, in 1692. Several young girls accused dozens of townspeople of witchcraft. The accused were jailed for months. Nineteen of them were eventually put to death. One 80-year-old man refused to admit his guilt at trial. He died when heavy stones were piled on top of his body. By 1700 the witch trials ended.

HANGMAN'S NOOSE

BAD MEDICINE

Almost from the time they landed in America, colonists battled new and deadly diseases. Smallpox, diphtheria, and yellow fever killed thousands. Smallpox attacked American Indians and colonists alike. After three or four days of fever, blisters broke out all over the body. Skin fell away, and the victims died in terrible pain. Diphtheria was a deadly lung disease. Yellow fever, spread by mosquitoes, caused high fever and death.

Doctors tried bleeding patients to cure these and other illnesses. A doctor made tiny cuts in the patient's arm until blood ran freely.

Doctors also gave foul-tasting medicines that caused vomiting or diarrhea. Doctors believed that blood, vomit, and diarrhea carried illnesses away.

For fever, colonial doctors cut fish called herrings down the back and tied them to their patients' feet. Other doctors gave patients a broth made of boiled toads. People believed that the stronger the smell, the better the medicine.

COLONIAL DOCTOR GATHERING PLANTS

Uncommon Cures

The women are pitifully tooth-shaken; whether through the coldness of the climate, or by sweetmeats [sugar], I am not sure. For toothache, I have found the following medicine very available – add butter to gunpowder and rub the jaw with it. For frozen limbs, make a lotion of soap, salt, and molasses or use cow dung boiled in milk.

John Josselyn, 1674

Colonists used hard soap and a washboard to do laundry.

WHAT'S THAT SMELL?

It wasn't just the medicines that smelled bad. Colonial people did too. They seldom bathed. Most people believed water was unhealthy. They thought the dirt and sweat caked into their skin protected them from illness. After finally taking a bath, one colonial woman said, "I bore it rather well, not having been wet all over for 28 years."

Most colonists had dirty hands, muddy feet, and greasy hair. Lice and nits crawled through colonists' hair and jumped from one person to another. Some colonists used fine combs to remove the nits. Others dusted their hair with powder. Most colonists just scratched.

Even so, people took great care to clean their clothes. Most only had two or three outfits, so keeping them clean wasn't easy. Women hauled water, heated it, and then scrubbed clothes by hand. During the winter, laundry piled up for weeks because the water froze. Most people were forced to wear dirty clothes covered with food splatters, animal droppings, and grime.

COLONIAL WATER BUCKET

DIFFICULT TIMES

Thanks to help from American Indian tribes, hearty colonists survived their first years in America. Indians taught colonists such useful skills as turning animal furs into clothing and carving dugout canoes. Even so, disputes arose over land and hunting grounds. When several Virginia tribes killed 347 colonists in 1622, colonists built forts and gathered weapons to protect themselves.

American Indians attacked small groups of settlers, using surprise as a weapon. Colonial leaders sought revenge without bothering to find out which tribe had attacked them or why. They struck out at the nearest village. Colonists used guns to kill the people and then destroyed their homes and crops.

In Massachusetts, colonists wiped out entire American Indian villages during the Pequot War of 1637. A few years later, in King Philip's War (1675-1676), American Indians burned colonial villages to the ground. Women and children were taken captive. Men were killed.

Disputes over land caused conflicts between colonists and American Indians.

TIMES CHANGE, SMELL REMAINS

Colonial life changed greatly in the years following the founding of Jamestown. Houses became larger. Many were built of brick. Brick houses didn't burn as easily as wood, and they lasted longer. Gardens flourished, and food was plentiful.

People still worked hard, but it was easier to find food and shelter. By the mid-1700s, there were stores, libraries, and mail service throughout the 13 colonies. Children attended schools. Stagecoaches carried people from place to place on well-worn roads. Newspapers provided current information.

But the colonies still smelled bad. People dumped their garbage in pits outside or burned it. Cows grazed on Boston Common. Pigs ran through the streets of New York City. Horses, cows, sheep, and chickens shared the streets with pigs and people.

Farm animals often roamed the streets of colonial towns.

Houses smelled of smoke and cooking odors. Even the fanciest homes did not have running water or indoor plumbing. Everyone used privies or outhouses, and most people still did not bathe.

Despite some smelly problems, the colonies were developing into a new country. In 1776 the 13 colonies declared their independence from Great Britain. They would soon become the United States of America.

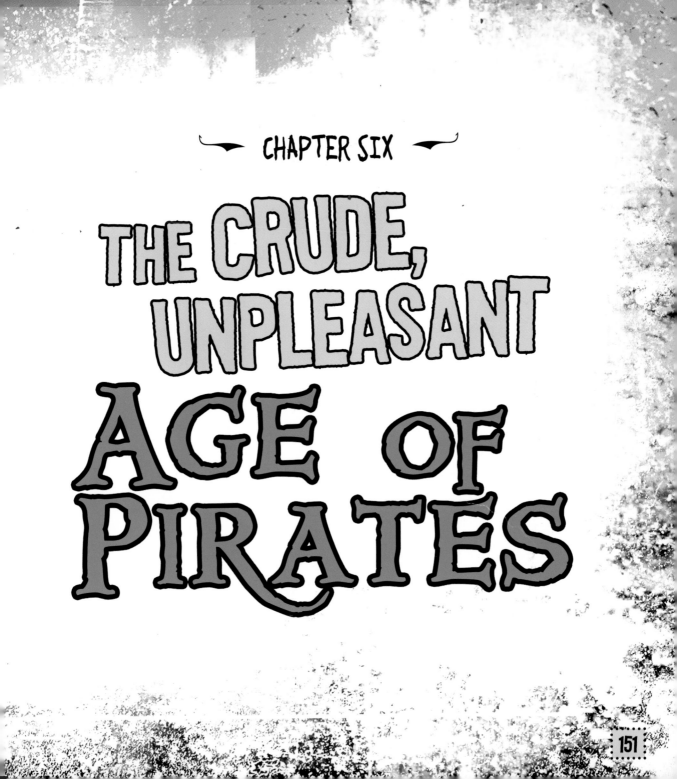

CHAPTER SIX

THE CRUDE, UNPLEASANT AGE OF PIRATES

THE GOLDEN AGE OF PIRATES
1690–1725

PAGE 168

LEGEND

● CITY
•••• TRADE ROUTE

0 — 600 MI
0 — 965 KM

N
W — E
S

1689

William Kidd earns the name pirate; the naming of Kidd as a pirate helps usher in the Golden Age of Pirates.

1693

An earthquake destroys the city of Port Royal in Jamaica; this city was a popular pirate hideout.

PIRATE CHAIN OF COMMAND

CAPTAIN—elected by pirate crew to command the ship

FIRST MATE—helped the captain run the ship

QUARTERMASTER—handled supplies, rations, and helped keep order on the ship

PILOT—kept the ship on course

SAILOR—general crewmember

1700

Jolly Roger flags become common on pirate ships.

1701

England's government takes William Kidd to court for charges of being a pirate; Kidd is put to death.

1702–1713

Queen Anne's War breaks out between France and England; at the end of the war sailors are out of work, and some become pirates.

PAGE 168

1714

New Providence in the Bahamas becomes a pirate hideout.

CAPTAIN BARTHOLOMEW ROBERTS

"No, a merry life and a short one shall be my motto."

as quoted in *Raiders and Rebels: The Golden Age of Piracy* by Frank Sherry

PAGE 167

1716

Edward Teach joins a pirate crew; Teach later becomes known as Captain Blackbeard.

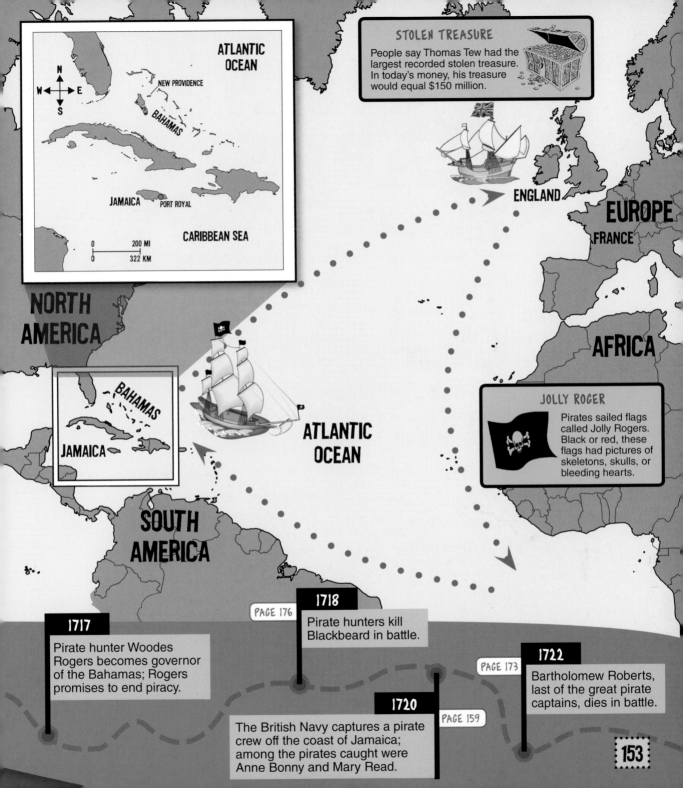

Inset Map (top left)

ATLANTIC OCEAN

N W E S

NEW PROVIDENCE

BAHAMAS

JAMAICA
PORT ROYAL

CARIBBEAN SEA

0 — 200 MI
0 — 322 KM

Map Labels

NORTH AMERICA

BAHAMAS

JAMAICA

SOUTH AMERICA

ATLANTIC OCEAN

ENGLAND

EUROPE

FRANCE

AFRICA

STOLEN TREASURE

People say Thomas Tew had the largest recorded stolen treasure. In today's money, his treasure would equal $150 million.

JOLLY ROGER

Pirates sailed flags called Jolly Rogers. Black or red, these flags had pictures of skeletons, skulls, or bleeding hearts.

Timeline

1717
Pirate hunter Woodes Rogers becomes governor of the Bahamas; Rogers promises to end piracy.

PAGE 176

1718
Pirate hunters kill Blackbeard in battle.

1720
The British Navy captures a pirate crew off the coast of Jamaica; among the pirates caught were Anne Bonny and Mary Read.

PAGE 159

PAGE 173

1722
Bartholomew Roberts, last of the great pirate captains, dies in battle.

A DEADLY CAREER

"Ahoy mate," orders a large man holding a sword. "To your post!" The smell of saltwater spray and seaweed fills the air as the large pirate ship readies to sail. Crowded onto the ship is a crew of dirty, sweaty men.

Each man moves about with a job to do. Some crewmembers struggle to pull up the ship's sails. Others blister their hands loosening ropes. Below the main deck, men move about in the dark. They stack barrels of food and water. As they work, rats scurry across the damp floor. Shouts fill the air as the ship's anchor lifts from the water. Moments later, the ship and its crew sail off on another treasure hunt.

For nearly 40 years, pirates ruled the seas. Often, pirates looked no different than people of their time. But make no mistake. These foul sailors surely did act different. Pirates made a living attacking ships, killing crews, and stealing treasure. If pirates were lucky, they lived long enough to spend their money. Unlucky pirates died at sea.

Danger filled pirates' lives. They lost limbs in battle and suffered fatal wounds. They also endured painful and deadly diseases. But weather was the greatest danger. Storms at sea damaged ships and killed crews. A pirate's life was crude and unpleasant. Still, their rough life often paid off with stolen treasure.

LIFE AT SEA

Hundreds of pirates were often crammed on a single ship. It didn't take long before foul smells filled the air. These men shared food, beds, and toilets. The few items they brought with them were kept in common chests shared by others.

No matter how watertight the ship, water filled the lower deck. Pirates dumped out the water as fast as they could. Still, they could not rid the ship of its foul sewer smell. The decks for food storage were a bit drier. But these decks had problems too. In these dark areas, barrels and sacks of food housed worms, spiders, and rats.

Captains had private quarters, but the crew's living space was tight. Pirates found any place they could to sleep. Some chose a sack of food as a restful spot. Others found a dry place on the rough wooden floor. Fires were not allowed below deck, so pirates spent many cold, damp nights trying to keep warm. During hot weather, the stench of sweat, waste, and salt water filled the ship.

RAT

FOUL FACT

To rid their ships of rats, pirates went hunting for the pests. A Spanish crew reported finding nearly 4,000 rats.

To make conditions even worse, pirates weren't alone below deck. Hundreds of rodents crawled over the sleeping men. Infections from rat bites sent many pirates to an early grave.

A FOUL CREW

After weeks at sea, pirates looked as foul as they smelled. Pirates had dirty hair and rotten, yellow teeth. On a pirate ship, brushing teeth and bathing rarely happened. Freshwater was saved for cooking and drinking.

Sweaty, dirty men added to the disgusting stench. Most pirates came on board a ship with only the clothes they were wearing. These clothes quickly became torn and full of bloodstains and sweat. Washing clothes helped, but pirates often only washed their shirts. A pirate's best chance at new clothes was to steal them from someone on another ship.

Picture the comfortable bathroom in your home. With one flush, waste disappears. Now picture a wooden board with some holes. That's what a pirate called a bathroom. Most pirates went to the bathroom using a simple hole in a board at the back of the ship. A pirate had to pick the right time for his bathroom stop. During rough waves, the waste sometimes fell onto the ship and onto other pirates. Yuck, watch out below!

Not all pirates were men. Anne Bonny and Mary Read dressed as men when they served aboard pirate ships.

Pirates' foul reputations matched the living quarters aboard their ships.

POOR DIET

A pirate's diet was far from fine dining. The men making meals on pirate ships were not trained cooks. These men were often crewmembers who had lost an arm or a leg in battle. They had no cooking skills and few supplies.

On a cramped ship, cooks did their best to feed hundreds of hungry men. Some ships had small kitchens. Other ships had no kitchens at all. Cooks made meals in large kettles over fires. On windy days, pirates did no cooking. One spark from a kettle fire could burn down the whole ship.

Before setting sail, pirates stocked up on vegetables and meat. But keeping food fresh was no easy task. Fresh food only lasted a few weeks. To help food last longer, cooks poured salt over vegetables and meat. As time went on, the food rotted. Cooks then used spices to hide the bad taste and served the rotten food anyway.

Wooden barrels kept food dry.

A cook on a pirate ship made meals with whatever supplies he could find.

Pirates raided towns for food and other supplies.

No Food in Sight

For these first took the leather, and sliced it in pieces. Then did they beat it between two stones, and rub it, often dipping it in the water of the river, to render it by these means supple and tender. Lastly, they scraped off the hair, and roasted or broiled it upon the fire.

Above quotation is based on the writing of Alexandre Olivier Exquemelin, as published in The Buccaneers of America, 1911.

Pirate ships sailed for weeks and months at a time. Their supplies did not last a whole voyage. Out at sea, pirates had several ways to restock their ship with food. They took food from the ships and towns they attacked. Pirates stopped at islands to hunt monkeys, birds, and turtles. They also fished for dolphins, tuna, and sea turtles.

Pirates ate a steady diet of hardtack. Made of flour and water, these hard biscuits didn't spoil as quickly as meat. Hardtack was a simple meal for ship cooks to prepare.

While hardtack was easy to keep, there were still a few problems. Hardtack quickly turned stale. Tiny bugs called weevils also found their way into these biscuits. But hungry pirates didn't care. They ate the hardtack, bugs and all.

On rare occasions, pirates had no food to eat. Cooks then had to make due with whatever they could find. When supplies were low, cooks used fish bones, animal bones, and even rats to make a nasty batch of bone soup.

HARDTACK

ARMED FOR BATTLE

Pirate ships carried deadly weapons. A single pirate ship often carried up to 40 cannons. Pirates had to be skilled when firing cannons. A misfire could give a pirate frightful burns and even take off an arm or a leg.

Fear was a pirate crew's best weapon. A raised flag or a warning shot were often enough to get another ship to surrender. When these warnings didn't work, pirate captains did not think twice to order an all-out attack. Some captains even ordered "no quarter." This order meant that pirates would fight to the death.

Boom! During attacks, pirates fired a volley onto the deck of the enemy ship. Pirates wanted to hurt the crew but not the ship. The volley sprayed glass, metal, or nails across the ship's deck. Unlucky crewmembers were left bloody and even blinded.

Pirates fired warning shots.

Pirates showed no mercy in battle. They would stop at nothing to get their treasure.

Painful volleys were often followed by grenades. These handmade bombs were dangerous. Once the bomb was lit, a pirate had only a matter of seconds before it blew. Pirates also threw stinkpots. They filled these clay pots with sulfur and rotten fish.

Pirates then muscled their way on ship in hand-to-hand battles. Pistols and muskets caused horrible injuries at close range. In most battles, pirates did not have much time to reload their guns. Once they fired, pirates turned their guns into clubs to strike their enemies. They also used cutlasses in close fighting. The sharp, curved edge of these swords cut deep, causing deadly wounds.

FOUL FACT

Blackbeard carried pistols, knives, and two swords with him at all times. He was one of the most feared pirates of the golden age.

PIRATE TREASURE

Pirates were willing to suffer disease, foul food, and deadly battles for one thing—treasure! Pirates captured ships and took their prized booty. In a pirate's world, almost anything was treasure. Pirates sold cloth, spices, and supplies for money. They even sold slaves. From anchors to rope, pirates stripped ships clean. Sometimes they even took the whole ship.

Beware! No one was safe when pirates went looking for treasure. Pirate crews sometimes held prisoners and whole towns for ransom. Pirates like Blackbeard showed no kindness. Stories say Blackbeard sliced off a man's finger just to get the man's diamond ring.

What did pirates do with their treasure? Few pirates, if any, buried their treasure. Most pirates sailed to hideouts. Port Royal, Jamaica, and New Providence in the Bahamas were favorite stops. Pirates felt at home in these wild ports. But they soon lost their money playing cards and dice.

Pirates divided their treasure once they made it to shore.

Not All Gold and Riches

The ship being taken, they found none in her what they thought ... All the treasure they got consisted only in fifty bars of iron, a small parcel of paper, some earthen jars full of wine, and other things of this kind; all of small importance.

Above quotation is based on the writing of Alexandre Olivier Exquemelin, as published in The Buccaneers of America, 1911.

BETTER NOT GET SICK!

Pirates had treasure, but what they really needed were doctors. On a pirate ship, a cook or carpenter became the ship doctor. These sailors had no medical training. They were chosen because they had a knife or saw. As ship doctors, they needed these tools to cut off injured arms and legs.

During battles, pirates suffered many injuries. With little medicine or clean water, wounds became infected. Arms and legs that did not heal were amputated. Often, the ship doctor had to cut off the limb within 24 hours of the injury.

A doctor used a red-hot saw or knife to remove the limb. The doctor hoped the heat of the knife or saw would stop the bleeding. If so, a pirate just might live. Of course, a pirate had to first make it through all the pain. There was no medicine, so pirates were awake through the entire operation.

FOUL FACT

Pirates who lost hands or legs often wore peg legs and hooks. Pirates made these tools from materials found on their ships.

On dirty ships, diseases spread quickly. Dysentery and smallpox wiped out pirate crews. Many more pirates suffered from scurvy. This painful disease gave pirates loose teeth, rotten gums, and bleeding under the skin. If left untreated, patients died. To stop scurvy, pirates drank ale with herbs. Later they learned to eat citrus fruit to prevent the disease.

On a pirate ship, many battle wounds turned deadly.

After many days at sea, tempers flared and fights broke out.

PIRATE CODES

After months at sea, pirates grew restless and often fought each other or their captain. It wasn't easy for a captain to keep order over a crew of men. Pirates were stuck together for many days. These hot, tired men often lashed out at each other.

Most pirate captains kept control by using fear and harsh punishments. Pirate codes helped captains run their ships. These codes were a strict set of rules pirates had to follow.

One of the most famous set of pirate codes was created by Bartholomew "Black Bart" Roberts. This fierce captain ruled a tight ship. His men could not gamble. Candles had to be put out at 8:00 each night. Pirates aboard Black Bart's ship had to follow the codes or risk injury and even death.

No matter the codes, each pirate captain had one idea in mind—controlling the ship. A captain's worst fear was mutiny. During a mutiny, unhappy pirates tried to rid a ship of its captain and his loyal crew. Some angry crews killed their captains. Others sent their captains out to sea in small boats with no food or water.

KEEPING ORDER

Life on a pirate ship was clear-cut. Pirates who followed the rules and fought in battles received rewards. Pirates who broke the rules faced terrible punishments.

On a pirate ship, even minor crimes had painful punishments. A pirate who took a lit candle below deck was flogged. The guilty pirate was whipped only once on the back. Left with a scar, the pirate would never forget this punishment.

A repeated crime or a serious crime could lead to keelhauling. For this punishment, a ship's crew tied a pirate to a rope. They lowered him into the water and dragged him under the ship. Sharp barnacles shredded the pirate's skin. His lungs quickly filled with water. Keelhauling was almost always deadly.

What's a punishment worse than death? Being marooned. An angry captain marooned a pirate on an island. These islands were often just sandbars, reefs, or stretches of empty land with no food or freshwater. The marooned pirate was given a bottle of water or rum and a pistol loaded with a single shot. Pirates could use the pistol to end their suffering. But many marooned pirates slowly starved to death. Others were swept away by the ocean tides.

Few marooned pirates lived to tell their story.

After Blackbeard was killed, British sailors hung his head from a ship's bow as a warning to other pirates.

GOLDEN AGE ENDS

During the golden age, pirates sailed the seas risking disease and death for treasure. But by the 1720s, their days were numbered. Navies around the world began to fight back against pirates.

Pirate hunters chased and captured pirates. At sea, navies attacked and destroyed pirate ships.

Captured pirates were quickly tried and hanged for their crimes. Town officials hung pirate bodies in ship harbors. These rotting bodies were a grim warning for pirates hoping to come ashore.

By the early 1800s, the life of pirates had changed. The pirates who once ruled the seas were now just outlaws on the run. They were no longer fierce hunters. Instead, pirates had become the hunted. Their captures and deaths brought an end to their golden age.

Even the feared pirate Blackbeard was killed by pirate hunters.

CHAPTER SEVEN

THE FOUL, FILTHY AMERICAN FRONTIER

THE AMERICAN FRONTIER
1841–1866

OREGON CITY, OR.

SUTTER'S FORT

PACIFIC OCEAN

MAY 1804

Explorers Meriwether Lewis and William Clark begin their journey across America to explore the West.

AMERICAN FRONTIER BY THE NUMBERS

500,000 – people who followed trails to the Western United States, 1840–1860

20,000 – number of people who died on the way west

2,000 – miles settlers traveled to get from Missouri to California or Oregon

1,600 – average number of pounds carried by a single wagon, including food and belongings

170 – average number of days it took settlers to travel west

1841

Oregon Trail traffic by pioneer farmers begins with the Bidwell-Bartleson Party of 71 people.

1846

Trail traffic increases with the addition of Mormon pioneers seeking religious freedom in Utah.

JULY 27, 1836

FROM THE DIARY OF NARCISSA WHITMAN, ONE OF THE FIRST WHITE WOMEN TO SETTLE WEST OF THE ROCKY MOUNTAINS

"We have plenty of dried buffalo meat, which we have purchased from the Indians — and dry it is for me. It appears so filthy! I can scarcely eat it; but it keeps us alive, and we ought to be thankful for it."

NOVEMBER 2, 1846

PAGE 194

The Donner Party is trapped by a snowstorm in the Sierra Nevada mountains. They are not rescued until February 1847.

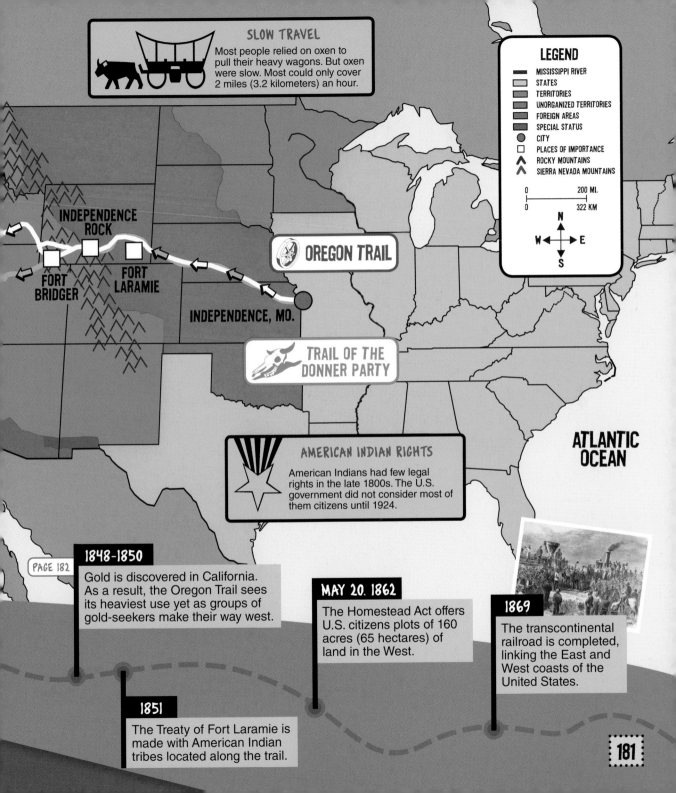

SLOW TRAVEL
Most people relied on oxen to pull their heavy wagons. But oxen were slow. Most could only cover 2 miles (3.2 kilometers) an hour.

LEGEND
— MISSISSIPPI RIVER
▢ STATES
▢ TERRITORIES
▢ UNORGANIZED TERRITORIES
▢ FOREIGN AREAS
▢ SPECIAL STATUS
● CITY
▢ PLACES OF IMPORTANCE
⋀ ROCKY MOUNTAINS
⋀ SIERRA NEVADA MOUNTAINS

0   200 MI.
0   322 KM

N
W   E
S

INDEPENDENCE ROCK

FORT BRIDGER

FORT LARAMIE

OREGON TRAIL

INDEPENDENCE, MO.

TRAIL OF THE DONNER PARTY

AMERICAN INDIAN RIGHTS
American Indians had few legal rights in the late 1800s. The U.S. government did not consider most of them citizens until 1924.

ATLANTIC OCEAN

PAGE 182

1848-1850
Gold is discovered in California. As a result, the Oregon Trail sees its heaviest use yet as groups of gold-seekers make their way west.

MAY 20, 1862
The Homestead Act offers U.S. citizens plots of 160 acres (65 hectares) of land in the West.

1869
The transcontinental railroad is completed, linking the East and West coasts of the United States.

1851
The Treaty of Fort Laramie is made with American Indian tribes located along the trail.

THE JOURNEY BEGINS

In the mid-1800s, many Americans were restless. Farmers longed for more land. Others hoped to find riches during the California gold rush. Some people went west in search of religious or social freedoms. Hoping for a better life, thousands of families crammed covered wagons full of food and belongings. They set out across the American frontier.

No one expected an easy trip. But many people weren't well enough to handle the trip. Sick people walked or rode in wagons, hoping for better health out west. Pregnant women followed their husband's dreams. They suffered from nausea and tiredness. Many women gave birth along the way.

During the day the pioneers sweated under the hot sun. They endured dust storms and swarms of mosquitoes. At night temperatures fell. Thunderstorms pounded pioneers with rain and hail.

Pioneers had to keep moving. Any delays could cause them to run out of food or be trapped in the snowy mountains. Despite the bitter cold and blistering heat, pioneers pushed on toward a new start in the West.

INSIDE OF A COVERED WAGON

Pioneer families loaded wagons and animals with belongings for the trip out west.

TOUGHING IT OUT

Westward caravans traveled at a steady pace to reach their destinations. Most pioneers made the journey west on foot. Many of them were barefoot. Passengers in a covered wagon only added weight for tired oxen to pull. The wagon's rocking motion and musty smells often made riders sick.

Some caravans struggled more than others. Some groups followed risky shortcuts. These unproven paths were often covered with trees and brush. Groups lost valuable travel time moving boulders and clearing new trails.

Pioneers walked across deserts, pushed their wagons up mountains, and waded through muddy rivers. It wasn't long before their pants and skirts were torn and filthy with dirt. Some travelers didn't even have a change of clothes for the journey.

FOUL FACT

Some historians believe that one in 10 travelers died during the journey west on the Oregon Trail.

Desert Crossing

We are traveling across a desert covered in prickly pears. My brothers and I don't wear shoes, and the prickly pear needles cut into our feet. It is our job to gather buffalo chips into a basket for building a fire later on. Each night, we are covered in dust. When the dry heat cracks and blisters our lips, we rub them with axle grease. Father says we will walk 15 miles each day.

Henry, age 10
May 1849

STOPS ALONG THE TRAIL

Each night, pioneers circled their wagons and made camp. But despite the open plains, travelers often found themselves surrounded by garbage left by other emigrants.

Travelers left behind rotting bodies of animals dead from starvation and exhaustion. Human and animal waste littered campsites. Empty supply bins and unwanted household items were scattered about. Heavy family heirlooms were tossed out.

Bathroom breaks were needed on the journey west. On the flat plains without a hill or tree in sight, no one had any real privacy. Men would use one side of the trail as a bathroom. Women would use the other side. Their long, full skirts provided some privacy during bathroom breaks on the trail.

COOKING WITH DUNG

Before leaving home, pioneers packed enough flour, sugar, salt, meat, and other goods to last about seven months. Along the way they'd use the supplies to make meals of baked bread, pancakes, and fried meat.

But as the journey grew longer, the meals got worse. If people didn't plan carefully, their food would run out. With few options, some people killed and ate their pack mules to survive. People boiled and ate buffalo hides. When food was really scarce, pioneers dined on leftover flour bags, boiled shoe leather, and even leather pants.

No matter what was on the menu, cooking on the trail was a dirty job. Some pioneers cooked on cast iron wood stoves. But many cooked over an open campfire.

COOKING POT

Travelers often cooked fresh game over open fires.

Little wood was available on the plains. Most fires were built over a pile of weeds and buffalo chips. As a result, the food typically had a lasting smell of smoke and dung. Campfires flared and food burned easily in the wind. When it rained it was impossible to keep a fire lit. If emigrants couldn't cook, they might be stuck eating raw bacon until the sun came out again.

WATER WORRIES

Traveling on hot, dusty trails made the pioneers dry with thirst. Clean water was often hard to find on the way west. Pioneers had no choice but to drink water made dirty by human and animal waste. It was either drink the foul water or die of dehydration.

People also had to deal with the bitter-tasting alkaline water that was common along the trails. They disguised the taste by making coffee. But people had to be careful. Strong alkaline water could kill humans, oxen, and other animals. The water could cause internal burns, stomach pain, and fever. Some victims even vomited blood.

Dying of thirst was a real possibility on the hot plains. Water was also a problem in colder weather if a caravan became trapped.

Livestock risked death without plenty of water on the trails.

FOUL FACT

Pioneers and livestock often drank water from the same containers.

DEADLY CONDITIONS

Every mile of the pioneers' journey seemed to hold new hardships. Wagons tipped over on steep mountain paths. Pioneers had to wade across swollen rivers. They risked drowning, losing their livestock or wagons, or sinking into hidden quicksand. Some pioneers and their livestock were swept away by raging rivers.

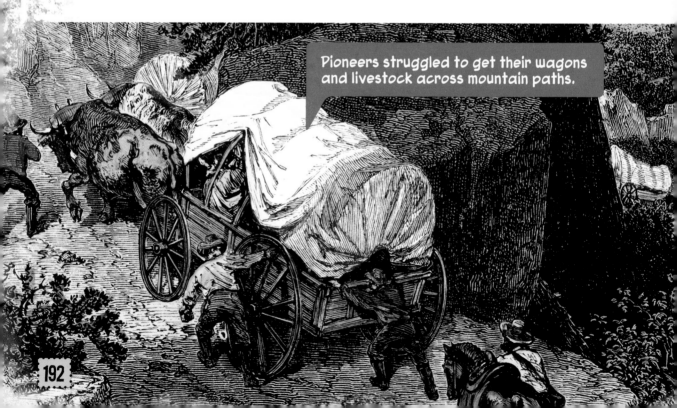

Pioneers struggled to get their wagons and livestock across mountain paths.

American Indians and pioneers sometimes joined together to hunt buffalo.

Emigrants also worried about running into American Indians. By the 1850s thousands of pioneers passed deadly diseases to Indian tribes. As more people came west, American Indians worried about losing their way of life. Some became angry. Some tribes attacked caravans in hopes of stopping settlers. But other American Indians acted as guides and traded goods with the pioneers.

THE DONNER PARTY

In May 1846, a group of 87 people and 23 wagons began the trip west. But it would be no ordinary journey. The Donner Party traveled slowly, took a risky shortcut, and crossed a stinging desert. In November 1846 a blizzard trapped the group in the Sierra Nevada mountains. Their supplies soon ran out. Some people starved to death. Others ate charred bones, twigs, bark, and leaves to survive.

A small group left camp to find help. They had little clothing or food. Soon the group was lost and out of food. Some starved to death. To survive the others ate the flesh of their dead companions.

Back at the campsite, the remaining members of the Donner Party ate mice and boiled tree branches. Still the months passed. Men, women, and children starved to death. The survivors began eating the dead. Only 46 members of the Donner Party survived. After the tragedy, volunteers organized West Coast Assistance and began searching for stranded emigrants each fall.

Desperate for Food

The little field mice that had crept into camp were caught then and used to ease the pangs of hunger. Also pieces of beef hide were cut into strips, singed, scraped, boiled to the consistency of glue, and swallowed with an effort; for no degree of hunger could make the saltless, sticky substance palatable. Marrowless bones which had already been boiled and scraped, were now burned and eaten, even the bark and twigs of pine were chewed in the vain effort to soothe the gnawings which made one cry for bread and meat.

Eliza P. Donner

DISEASE AND DEATH

Even when a wagon train was traveling on schedule, conditions were uncomfortable. Nearly every emigrant suffered from dysentery or diarrhea. Scurvy, caused by a lack of vitamin C, was also common. Victims had leg pain and bleeding gums. Cholera was one of the most feared diseases and also the most common. It caused vomiting and diarrhea and could kill within hours.

Pioneers couldn't do much to avoid disease or cure their ills. Sickness was treated with herbs, peppermint, rum, and whiskey. Sick travelers often became too weak to walk and had to ride in the cramped, stuffy wagon.

When disease didn't strike, accidents remained a serious threat. Buffalo stampedes trampled anyone in their paths. Rattlesnakes bit and poisoned their victims. People fell from moving wagons, sometimes getting crushed to death under the wheels.

GRAVE SITUATIONS

Many pioneers didn't survive the trip west. When someone died, family members struggled with what to do with the body. The ground was too hard to dig a deep grave. There wasn't always time to build a coffin. Bodies were sometimes placed in a shallow grave without a coffin. Other bodies were simply covered with a pile of rocks.

When people knew they were dying on the trails, they worried about what would happen to their remains. They begged their families to protect them from grave robbers or hungry wolves.

Sometimes people carried a dead body with them rather than bury it in a spot they couldn't visit. Musty, strong-smelling camphor was sprinkled on the body and clothing to mask the scent of decay. One man traveling from Missouri to Oregon pickled a family member's body in a tub of whiskey for the trip.

FILTHY HOMESTEADS

Once pioneers arrived out west, their hard work wasn't over. They needed shelter. Settlers in Oregon and California built log cabins or lived in tents.

Rather than continue west, some settlers made homes on the Great Plains. On these grasslands, logs weren't easy to find. Settlers there created dugouts and built homes made of sod. Hay on the floor helped warm sod homes in winter, but it also attracted fleas. Snakes and mice lived in the walls. When a sod roof was dry, dirt would sprinkle into the house. In rainy weather, the roof would leak muddy water.

Without indoor plumbing, a pioneer family needed an outhouse, which would serve as a toilet. This small building had a bench inside. A hole in the bench opened over a deep pit dug into the ground. The outhouse could be smelly, so a small window was cut at the top of the door.

SOD HOUSE

Pioneer children pitched in to start new lives in the West. Both girls and boys plowed fields, cleaned chicken coops, milked cows, and trapped wild animals to eat. Dinner might include antelope, raccoon, or rabbit meat. Some children skinned their catches and sold the fur to earn money for their families.

Pioneer women often had to hunt for and prepare food.

SEARCH FOR FOOD

The search for food didn't end once settlers arrived in the West. Men hunted wild game for food. But meat spoiled quickly on a hot day. Settlers smoked, dried, and salted meat to prevent rotting. The meat tasted good, but it was tough to chew. People often compared it to shoe leather.

Settlers knew they risked developing scurvy if they didn't eat fruits and vegetables. These foods were also preserved to last through the winter. Some settlers didn't have containers for storage, so they used old kerosene cans. The cans were reused until someone noticed the food inside tasted like tin or had turned black.

Drinking water was another priority. Some people collected rainwater in barrels and pans. Before drinking it they'd skim off the flies, mosquitoes, and dust that collected on top of the water. Others dug a well near their house. They had to choose the well site carefully. Otherwise water would be made dirty by human and animal waste.

NEW DANGERS

On the frontier, pioneer families continued to struggle. Great Plains settlers worried about prairie fires, tornadoes, and dust storms that filled the air with brown grit. During winter wild blizzards covered their small homes with snow and ice. Settlers strung ropes from the house to the barn, so no one would be lost in a blizzard.

On the plains and in the western states, mothers treated injuries and illnesses as best they could. They had no help from trained doctors. They tried to keep their children safe from wild animals like rattlesnakes and mountain lions. They feared attack by American Indians, although many Indians were friendly. Indians shared food, like a bread made with crickets and dried acorns.

Settlers struggled to build new communities on the rugged frontier. They built churches and one-room schools. But building materials weren't always available. Sometimes children learned their lessons in a boxcar, sheep wagon, tent, or chicken house.

Prairie fires threatened homes and crops.

With the journey behind them, the settlers could build new lives. Some stayed put. Many struck out again, moving farther and farther west. They were pioneers eager to explore new places and opportunities before settling down for good.

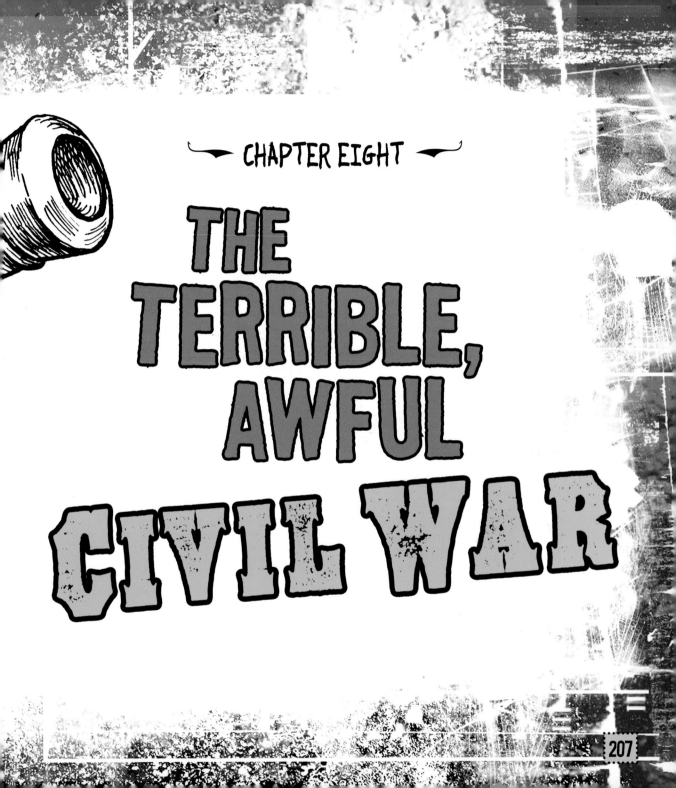

CHAPTER EIGHT

THE TERRIBLE, AWFUL CIVIL WAR

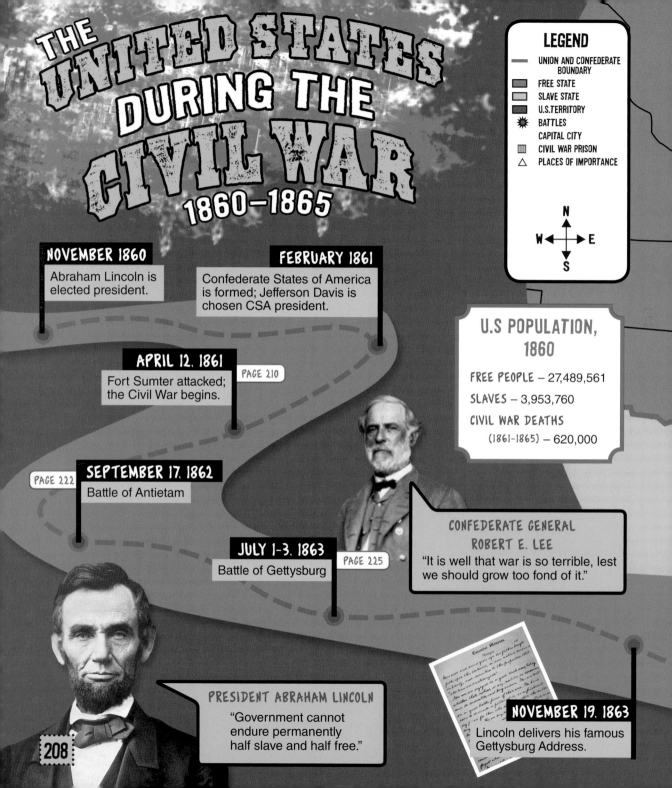

THE UNITED STATES DURING THE CIVIL WAR 1860–1865

LEGEND
— UNION AND CONFEDERATE BOUNDARY
▭ FREE STATE
▭ SLAVE STATE
▭ U.S. TERRITORY
✸ BATTLES
CAPITAL CITY
▥ CIVIL WAR PRISON
△ PLACES OF IMPORTANCE

N W E S

NOVEMBER 1860
Abraham Lincoln is elected president.

FEBRUARY 1861
Confederate States of America is formed; Jefferson Davis is chosen CSA president.

APRIL 12, 1861
Fort Sumter attacked; the Civil War begins.
PAGE 210

U.S POPULATION, 1860
FREE PEOPLE – 27,489,561
SLAVES – 3,953,760
CIVIL WAR DEATHS
(1861–1865) – 620,000

PAGE 222
SEPTEMBER 17, 1862
Battle of Antietam

JULY 1–3, 1863
Battle of Gettysburg
PAGE 225

CONFEDERATE GENERAL ROBERT E. LEE
"It is well that war is so terrible, lest we should grow too fond of it."

PRESIDENT ABRAHAM LINCOLN
"Government cannot endure permanently half slave and half free."

NOVEMBER 19, 1863
Lincoln delivers his famous Gettysburg Address.

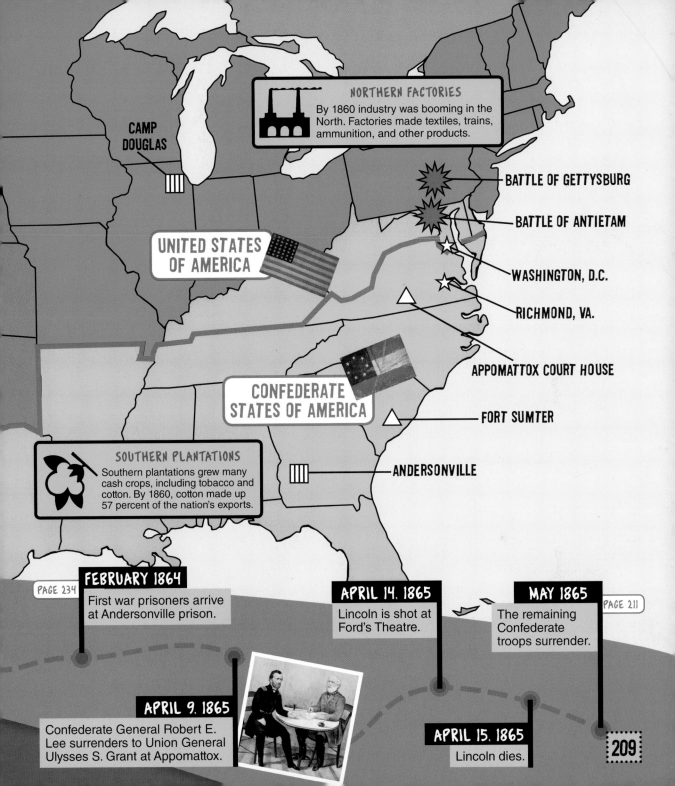

NORTHERN FACTORIES
By 1860 industry was booming in the North. Factories made textiles, trains, ammunition, and other products.

CAMP DOUGLAS

UNITED STATES OF AMERICA

BATTLE OF GETTYSBURG

BATTLE OF ANTIETAM

WASHINGTON, D.C.

RICHMOND, VA.

APPOMATTOX COURT HOUSE

CONFEDERATE STATES OF AMERICA

FORT SUMTER

ANDERSONVILLE

SOUTHERN PLANTATIONS
Southern plantations grew many cash crops, including tobacco and cotton. By 1860, cotton made up 57 percent of the nation's exports.

PAGE 234

FEBRUARY 1864
First war prisoners arrive at Andersonville prison.

APRIL 14, 1865
Lincoln is shot at Ford's Theatre.

MAY 1865
The remaining Confederate troops surrender.

PAGE 211

APRIL 9, 1865
Confederate General Robert E. Lee surrenders to Union General Ulysses S. Grant at Appomattox.

APRIL 15, 1865
Lincoln dies.

THE WAR BEGINS

During the U.S. Civil War (1861-1865), eager young soldiers marched off to fight for Union or Confederate armies. These proud men wanted to defend their countries. But army life was filled with death, disease, and foul living conditions.

The war began on April 12, 1861, when Confederate troops fired cannons at Fort Sumter. When Union troops at the fort surrendered, cheers rang out in southern streets. Both sides were ready to defend their way of life. Most thought the war would be over by Christmas.

Northerners were quick to join the Union army. Pro-Union people favored a strong federal government. Most were generally opposed to slavery.

WOUNDED UNION SOLDIER

ATTACK ON FORT SUMTER, SOUTH CAROLINA

Southerners had opposed Abraham Lincoln for president. Southerners believed states' rights were most important and that slavery was a way of life. Lincoln's election started the secession of 11 states.

When the fighting ended in May 1865, weary soldiers returned home to a changed nation. Many men limped on a leg and a crutch. No one was ever the same again.

TATTERED UNIFORMS

How would you like to go to school wearing a scratchy jacket, tattered pants, and worn shoes? That's just what Civil War soldiers wore whether they were marching, fighting, eating, or sleeping.

Uniforms for both sides were often in short supply. In the South, the government didn't make enough uniforms for all the soldiers. Confederate soldiers wore their regular clothes and parts of army uniforms.

Union soldiers were itchy all over thanks to uniforms made of rough, scratchy fabrics. Soldiers had no coats, gloves, or hats to protect them during winter.

Union soldiers wore blue uniforms while the uniforms of Confederate troops were gray.

Soldiers' uniforms quickly looked like dirty rags. Uniforms became stiff and stinky from sweat. Jackets and pants were ripped, dirty, and spotted with blood. Uniforms were rarely washed. Underwear? Soldiers didn't change or wash their underwear for months at a time. Soldiers seldom received replacement clothing, so they took jackets, pants, or boots off the dead.

Socks protected a soldier's feet. But a soldier's socks went unwashed for weeks or months. They soon became stiff and filled with germs. As the war dragged on, soldiers wore their boots with bare feet. When boots wore out, soldiers wrapped their feet in rags and kept on marching.

HARD GROUND, WET BEDROLLS

Sleeping outside might sound like fun to you, but for Civil War soldiers it was miserable. Little protected them from rain, snow, or summer heat. Even less protected them from pesky mosquitoes and body lice. Mosquitoes buzzed and bit all night long. Lice infested soldiers' bedrolls, clothing, beards, and hair.

Lucky soldiers slept in canvas tents with dirt floors. Other soldiers slept on the ground on bedrolls. These blankets were rolled up and carried on the soldiers' backs while they marched. If the ground was wet or if rain fell at night, bedrolls became soggy and muddy.

Crowded, filthy living quarters were great for bacteria and germs. Diarrhea was a common complaint for soldiers. They also suffered pneumonia, typhoid, cholera, and tuberculosis.

Civil War soldiers spent many cold nights sleeping outdoors on the ground.

FOUL FACT

Some soldiers slept in open-air beds made by piling hay or straw between two logs.

TEETH DULLERS

Think school lunches are bad? Try dining on stale, moldy crackers day after day. Hoping for some meat with your meal? Look closer at the crackers. Those small specks are maggots. Sound disgusting? Maybe so, but hardtack crackers were standard food for Civil War soldiers.

Hardtack was made from flour, salt, and water. It was light and easy to carry. The salt in hardtack helped soldiers to sweat, which kept them from fainting in the heat.

Hardtack crackers were called "teeth dullers" and "iron plate biscuits" because they were so hard. "Worm castle" was another name for hardtack because it often was full of weevils and maggots. Some soldiers dipped their hardtack in hot coffee to soften it and kill the worms. Others went ahead and ate the worms.

Meat was scarce for soldiers. Depending on what was available, soldiers ate the meat of cows, horses, mules, and even rats. Salt helped preserve meat. But often the meat was rotten.

HARDTACK

A diet of hardtack and salted meat left soldiers constantly thirsty. The water they drank came from nearby streams, ponds, and lakes. Drinking dirty water caused soldiers to develop dysentery and other diseases.

ON THE MARCH

Civil War soldiers did most of their traveling on foot. One Union soldier marched 143 miles (230 km) in 16 days, with a two-day battle in between. That's a lot of ground to cover in worn-out boots, no socks, and blistered toes.

Soldiers marched 15 to 20 miles (24 to 32 km) a day. But hot weather made long marches risky. Soldiers who wore wool uniforms and carried bedrolls, food, and guns often fainted when marching on hot days.

Weary from travel, soldiers marched into battle.

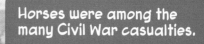

Horses were among the many Civil War casualties.

The Army of the Potomac marched 20 to 30 miles (32 to 48 km) a day from Virginia to Gettysburg in June 1863. Many of these men suffered sunstroke.

Other than the soldiers' blistered feet, horses were the main transportation during the war. Up to 2 million horses pulled wagons, carried riders, and braved bullets on Civil War battlefields.

FOUL FACT

In a single day, 1 million Civil War horses would have peed enough urine to fill more than 12 standard swimming pools.

DEADLY WEAPONS

Why were the battles of the Civil War so horribly bloody? Civil War soldiers were armed with rifles. Rifles were accurate at much farther distances than past weapons. The newer weapons had a closer **range**. Their rifles shot lead bullets that exploded when they hit bone. But soldiers still had to advance near enemies to drive them off the battlefield. The closer the bullet's impact, the more damage it caused.

These rifles could crush an advancing enemy as they did during the Battle of Antietam. On September 17, 1862, in Maryland, Union soldiers marched shoulder to shoulder, creating a wall of men. Confederate soldiers, lying in a nearby cornfield, suddenly stood up and fired. Union soldiers went down in waves. Antietam was the bloodiest single day in the Civil War. Close to 23,000 men were killed, wounded, or captured.

Battle Wounds

Thomas Hains of Company E took off his hat, placed it on his ramrod, and holding it up, shouted to the boys along the line to see what a close call he had had while out in front, for a minie ball had passed through the creased crown of his hat, making four holes. Before he could get his hat back on his head, a small shell burst over us and mortally wounded him.

Sergeant Alexander G. Downing
Confederate Army
Sunday, April 5, 1862

FOUL FACT

Metal shells exploded in air. They rained down sharp pieces of metal, killing large numbers of soldiers.

Soldiers for both the North and South suffered heavy losses at Gettysburg.

Minie balls were the most common ammunition used. These lead balls caused about 108,000 battlefield wounds. Head shots killed instantly. Stomach shots were usually fatal too.

During the Battle of Gettysburg in July 1863, Confederate troops were mowed down by gunfire as they advanced during Pickett's Charge. Soldiers lay where they fell with large holes in their stomachs.

Arms and legs hit with minie balls were often amputated. Shattered bones could not be put back together. Wounded soldiers made a tourniquet from a belt, rope, or shirtsleeve to stop the bleeding.

If ammunition ran out, soldiers used bayonets at the end of their guns to attack the enemy. Bayonets sliced through uniforms. Germs from the dirty uniforms were plunged deep into the victim's body. Infected wounds killed many soldiers long after the battle.

BATTLING GERMS

Imagine being a Civil War soldier on the march for hours under a hot sun. Your stomach is churning. That bacon you ate last night smelled bad, but you ate it anyway. Now you feel like your guts might explode. At last the commanding officer shouts, "Take 10," and you rush to the nearest bush.

After, you hurry down to the pond below to wash. Then you take off your sweaty hat, fill it with pond water and drink. "Fall in," the officer shouts, and you march off again.

People were unaware of germs in the 1860s. Disease spread easily in war conditions. The sicker soldiers got, the worse their living conditions became. If soldiers washed at all, they did it in the same water they drank.

In the 1860s some people, even doctors, believed that full beards protected men from sickness. But the opposite was true. Spit, vomit, and blood stuck to moustaches and beards. Lice often made their homes in the long beards.

A Confederate soldier's sewing kit included a toothbrush and washcloth.

Civil War soldiers often bathed in murky river water.

By 1863 living conditions for Union soldiers became so bad that generals began issuing hygiene orders. Men were ordered to wear their hair short and bathe twice a week. They were to change clothes at least once a week. But soldiers often ignored these orders.

PILES OF WASTE

Picture yourself living in a camp with hundreds of men and piles of waste all around. Pretty stinky, huh? During the Civil War, human and animal waste piled up around army camps, hospitals, and prisons. Keeping clean was an impossible task.

Union and Confederate soldiers dug trenches to use as latrines. These stinky dirt pits were often dug close to the camp's water and food supply. If the waste wasn't covered with a layer of dirt daily, flies became a serious problem. Flies feeding on waste brought germs to the camp food supplies. Rain washed the waste into the ground, where it mixed with the water supply.

Field hospitals were almost as bad as the camps. These temporary hospitals were set up in tobacco storehouses, animal barns, large tents, or even in the open air. Doctors and nurses seldom washed their hands between caring for the wounded men. When they did wash, it was often with water contaminated from nearby latrines.

Surrounded by Waste

We find about the grounds, an area of over three acres, encircling the camp as a broad belt, on which is deposited an almost perfect layer of human excrement [waste].

A sanitary inspector, describing "Camp Misery," a camp for wounded soldiers in Alexandria, Virginia.

SAWBONES

For a Civil War soldier, the field hospital was more dreaded than the battle itself. These temporary hospitals were hastily set up near battlefields. Doctors often had few supplies and little or no clean water. Bare, bloody ground was the only bed for most of the wounded soldiers.

Civil War doctors treated soldiers for many illnesses. Diarrhea was the most common, and deadly, disease. More Civil War soldiers died from diarrhea than were killed in battle.

More than 70 percent of the patients treated had injuries to their arms or legs. Amputation was the most common treatment for wounded soldiers. Amputations were done with little or no anesthesia. Seriously wounded men in the field waited for hours, sometimes days, for treatment. Doctors stood for hours, sawing through bones. This method of amputation gave Civil War doctors the nickname "sawbones."

Union soldiers tend to a wounded man in 1861.

Doctors treating the injured did not know about bacteria and germs. They treated patient after patient without first washing their hands or their instruments. Civil War doctors wore bloodstained coats as they tended to patients. Bloody bandages and sponges used to wash wounds were rinsed out in buckets of dirty water and reused.

SURGEON'S AMPUTATION KIT

PRISON HORRORS

Life on the battlefield or in field hospitals was horrible. But nothing compared to the horrors suffered by prisoners of war. Men captured in or after a battle were sent to prison camps.

Camps were crammed full of prisoners. Sick and healthy men lived together in filthy conditions. Flies, bugs, maggots, and lice lived on the soldiers.

Starvation was a daily threat for prisoners. An army that could barely feed its soldiers cared little about feeding enemy prisoners. What food prisoners got was often unfit to eat. Food was simply dumped on the filthy ground. Prisoners fought each other for every scrap.

Beds were seldom provided for prisoners. Most men slept outdoors. They had nothing to protect them from the weather.

Lack of fresh fruits and vegetables led many war prisoners to get scurvy. Scurvy victims could not chew any solid food. Their gums became black and rotten.

Men at Civil War prison camps suffered through miserable living conditions.

FOUL FACT

Civil War prisoners often caught dogs and rats to eat.

Outnumbered guards feared prison escapes. They allowed only a few inmates to go to the latrines at any one time. Many inmates waited two or more days for the chance to go. Prisoners lived in pools of their own waste.

The Confederacy's Andersonville is the most infamous of all Civil War prisons. In all, about 33,000 Union soldiers found themselves in Andersonville at some point during the Civil War. More than 13,000 men died at this camp in Georgia.

A wooden fence surrounded the camp, but it was almost unneeded. A line around the prison marked the boundary for prisoners. A single finger across this deadline was enough to get a prisoner shot on the spot.

But cruel treatment of prisoners was not limited to the Confederates. Camp Douglas in Chicago was considered the North's Andersonville. Hunger and disease plagued inmates here as well. To prevent their escape, prisoners were not allowed to wear clothes. Even blankets were taken away. Many Confederates imprisoned at Camp Douglas froze to death.

ANDERSONVILLE PRISON CAMP, 1864

Disease and Despair

There are millions and millions of all kinds of vermin here, flies, bugs, maggots and lice, some of them as large as spiders. If they once get the best of you, you are a goner. A great many of the prisoners are hopelessly crazy, starvation, disease and vermin being the cause ... I am somewhat crippled, myself, but I manage to try and wash and keep clean, that is the principal thing. One hundred have died within the last 24 hours.

Michael Dougherty
Teenage Union Soldier imprisoned at Andersonville
May 1864

PHOTO CREDITS

BIBLIOGRAPHY

Page 11—from *Ancient Near Eastern Texts Relating to the Old Testament*, edited by James B. Pritchard (Princeton, N.J.: Princeton University Press, 1955) and reprinted in *Everyday Life in Ancient Egypt* by Lionel Casson (Baltimore: Johns Hopkins University Press, 2001); Page 31—from *Ancient Records of Egypt; Historical Documents from the Earliest Times to the Persian Conquest, collected, edited, and translated, with commentary by James Henry Breasted.* Chicago: The University of Chicago Press, 1906-07); Page 51—as published in *De Medicina* by Aulus Cornelius Celsus (Cambridge, Mass.: Harvard University Press, 1935–38); Page 58—from *The Deeds of the Divine Augustus* by Augustus, as published in *The Gladiators: History's Most Deadly Sport* by Fik Meijer and translated by Liz Walters (New York: Thomas Dunne Books, 2005); Page 69—from *The Excruciating History of Dentistry: Toothsome Tales and Oral Oddities from Babylon to Braces* by James Wynbrandt (New York: St. Martin's Press, 1998); Page 89—from *The Decameron* by Giovanni Boccaccio as published in *Decameron/ Giovanni Boccaccio,* translated from the Italian and introduced by J. G. Nichols (New York: Everyman's Library/ Alfred A. Knopf, 2009); Page 103—from the *Ynglinga Saga* by Snorri Sturluson as published in *The Viking World* by Jacqueline Simpson (New York: St. Martin's Press, 1980); Page 119—from *Beowulf,* translated by John McNamara (New York: Barnes and Noble, Inc., 2005); Page 129—based on the writing of Thomas Prince, as published in *The Annals of New England, 1726,* and quoted in *Woman's Life in Colonial Days* by Carl Holliday (Mineola, N.Y.: Dover, 1999); Page 137—as published in *Children in Colonial America* edited by James Marten (New York: New York University Press, 2007); Page 143— from *The American Heritage History of the Thirteen Colonies* by Louis B. Wright (New York: American Heritage, 1967); Pages 162 and 169—as published in *The Buccaneers of America* by A. O. Exquemelin, Henry Powell, and Basil Ringrose (New York: The MacMillan Company, 1911); Page 185— from *Frontier Children* by Linda Peavy and Ursula Smith (Norman, Okla.: University of Oklahoma Press, 1999); Page 195—as published in *The Expedition of the Donner Party and its Tragic Fate* by Eliza P. Donner Houghton (Lincoln, Neb.: University of Nebraska Press, 1997); Page 223—from *Downing's Civil War Diary* by Alexander G. Downing and Olynthus Burroughs Clark (The Historical Department of Iowa, 1916); Page 229—as published in *Doctors in Blue: The Medical History of the Union Army in the Civil War* by George Worthington Adams (New York: H. Schuman, 1952); Page 235—from *Reluctant Witnesses: Children's Voices from the Civil War* by Emmy E. Werner (Boulder, Colo.: Westview Press, 1998).

INDEX

INDEX